Shadow Prayers
Reflections from a Pandemic Year

Gary Allison Furr

Shadow Prayers: Reflections from a Pandemic Year
ISBN: Softcover 978-1-955581-45-5
Copyright © 2022 by Gary Allison Furr

All rights reserved. No part of this book may be reproduced or transmitted in any form or by any means, electronic or mechanical, including photocopying, recording, or by any information storage and retrieval system, without permission in writing from the publisher.

Parson's Porch Books is an imprint of Parson's Porch *&* Company (PP*&*C) in Cleveland, Tennessee. PP*&*C is an innovative organization which raises money by publishing books of noted authors, representing all genres. Its face and voice is **David Russell Tullock** (dtullock@parsonsporch.com).

Parson's Porch *&* Company *turns books into bread & milk* by sharing its profits with the poor.

www.parsonsporch.com

Shadow Prayers

Endorsements

Beloved and brilliant Birmingham pastor, Gary Furr, recounts the year of the pandemic, teaching us how to grieve and reflect through each of his poems and prayers, haikus and song. Through his psalm-like collection of writings, he captures the melancholy and mourning of the year of 2020, while simultaneously holding a lantern for a way forward, for today and years to come.

– Jenny Eaton Dyer, PhD, The 2030 Collaborative

Gary Furr is a creative pastor and an effective Christian leader, and he has come up with an original idea for a book. He has created a record of things that he said to his congregation in Birmingham during the first year of the Covid-19 pandemic which happens to have been the last year before his retirement. He organized the book according to the ancient Christian calendar. Each of the eight liturgical seasons begins with a paragraph of explanation about the season, two haiku, and a short list of developments in the pandemic during that period. These are followed by selected sermons, meditations, prayers, poetry, and original songs that Gary presented during that season. The result is a colorful mosaic of Christian wisdom and encouragement written in language that is unfailingly fresh. A major thread running through his ministry during that dark year is Christian hope which, like rain, "finds every leaf and gives it a drink."

—Fisher Humphreys, Professor of Divinity, Emeritus, Samford University

Dr. Gary Furr claims his "mind is like an entire cage full of monkeys on steroids." Don't take the joke. Here is authentic, pandemic-produced piety that stills the soul. It is a reminder of the spiritual gifts imposed by the virus: silence and solitude, a lighter load, new visions and innovations, and our aching, throbbing need for each other. Read it slowly. You will stop often, sometimes lingering long, to ponder your existence, to confront your moral shortfall, to pray for a nurse, or to remember the wall-to-wall pain in our world. They should have taught us to pray like this in seminary.

—Walter B. Shurden, Minister-at-Large at Mercer University

The timelines in each section come from a ***Washington Post*** article, "Sorrow and Stamina, Defiance and Despair: It's Been a Year," by Reis Thebault, Tim Meko and Junne Alcantara, on March 11, 2021. Hopefully it helps to set the tumultuous events of the year against the backdrop of the larger setting of what was happening in the world. While we all moved through that time, it was such a chaotic time that it is easy to forget just how rapidly events were moving from month to month. Perhaps this will help.

The introductions to the sections of the church liturgical year are based on summaries appearing in Hardin, Quillian and White, ***The Celebration of the Gospel: A Study in Christian Worship***, (Abingdon Press, 1964), and Wetzler and Huntingdon, ***Seasons & Symbols: A Handbook On the Church Year*** (Minneapolis: Augsburg Publishing), although I have rephrased and summarized the material in my own way.

Music lyrics that I have utilized come from the album, ***Flat Tire On Memory Lane*** by myself and Mark Weldon, released in 2020. All lyrics are mine. The music is available on the website https://gafurr.com Some materials appeared originally in the Vestavia Hills Baptist Church newsletter, ***VHBC Connections*** and other materials were originally posted on my blog, "The Flatpicking Pilgrim's Progress," https://garyfurr.me

I want to thank LaMon Brown for editing this material and offering helpful suggestions and for friends who read this manuscript. I always appreciate David Tullock and Parson's Porch for their excellent work in getting my publication done so effectively.

I dedicate this book to my grandchildren, Georgia, Eva Kate, Zadie, and Wallena. At the time that I write this they are the delight of my life and are all children enough still to have retained the joy of play and imagination. It is to them and their future that this volume is lovingly dedicated.

Contents

Introduction 13

Lent

Transmission 19
Blurred Lines 20
March 2020 Timeline 21
The Gift of Life 23
The Storm Begins 25
Pastoral Prayer March 1, 2020 29
Blessing at the Chamber of Commerce March 10. 2020 30
Pastoral Prayer Sunday, March 15, 2020. 31
Pastoral Prayer April 1, 2020 32
Pontius Pilate..34
Atticus 35
Webinarious..36

Holy Week

Erosion..39
On a Vent 40
Living and Dying Alone 41
Faces 45
Coming Through 47
Walking Around Jerusalem 48
Good Friday 50
Preaching Alone...51

Easter

Change..55
Walking 56
Pastoral Prayer, Easter Sunday April 8, 2020 57
Thunderstorm 59
Authority 60
Lost...61
Pastoral Prayer, Youth Sunday, April 20, 2020 62
Loving God, ...62
Poor Virus 64
Pastoral Prayer May 6, 2020 65
Untold Tales from the Exile 67
Pastoral Prayer Memorial Day, Sunday, May 29, 1994 68

Pentecost

Ground Zero 73
Quarantine 74

May-June 2020 Timeline 75
The Crucifixion.. 76
From My Newsletter Column After the Killing Of George Floyd. 77
A Prayer for the World God Loves.. 79
From Here to Okay... 81
Communion Prayer June 24, 2020 83
A Prayer for the Nation July 4, 2020 84
Shields of Fear.. 86

Ordinary Time

Politifusing... 89
Connectivity 90
A Prayer for Trust August 1, 2020 91
Stuck in the Mud 93
Pastoral Prayer August 12, 2020.. 94
Pastoral Prayer August 19, 2020.. 96
Dust Storm 98
Repent 99
Opening 100
Pastoral Prayer August 25, 2020... 101
Pastoral Prayer September 9, 2020 102
Frank Lloyd Wright.. 104
Pastoral Prayer September 16, 2020 105
Pastoral Prayer October 7, 2020... 107
Pastoral Prayer in Stewardship Season October 14, 2020 109
Pastoral Prayer Children's' Sabbath Sunday, October 21, 2020................ 110
Quiet: A Reflection 112
Empty Spaces.. 114
November 2020 Timeline 115
Pastoral Prayer All Saints Sunday, November 2020................................... 116
I Hope We'll Be Together.. 117
Living Memory... 118
The Desecration of Mussolini 119

Advent

New Normal.. 123
Waiting 124
Stars and Stripes... 125
Pastoral Prayer Advent, December 1, 2020 127
Pastoral Prayer *Advent 3* December 12, 2020.. 129

Christmas

Web of Fear	133
Nature Breathes	134
My Last Christmas Eve	135
Pastoral Prayer January 4, 2021	137

Epiphany

Selfies	141
Childhood Regrets	142
"Choice Words"	143
Resignation Letter	150
Pastoral Prayer January 17, 2021, MLK Holiday Weekend	153
Martin Luther King Day, January 18, 2021	155
McDonald's Drive-Through January 20, 2021	158
Pastoral Prayer The Spiritual Journey January 24, 2021	159
Pastoral Prayer for Guidance January 31, 2021	161
Pastoral Prayer February 7, 2021	163
"Love One Another"	165
Heaven's Gate	172
Every Time I Think of You	174
My Final Column	175
Farewell	177

Introduction

This is a collection of poems, prayers and lyrics written in 2020 and 2021. That it was a time of global pandemic is understood, since that was the universal experience of all of us who lived through that time. But I mention that in case someone reads this volume years from now.

I am a writer, but I would not consider myself a great poet. I do love words—their sounds and rhythms, and possibilities. I am a musician but not a very well-known one. There is something about marrying word and emotional tone through music that satisfies me. I am a preacher, but not a famous preacher, though I have never considered that something anyone should aspire to, even as many seem to have done so! The temptations of sin and ego are as rampant in the institutional ministry as everywhere else in humanity—perhaps even more deadly since we have so much motivation to lie to ourselves and others about it. So, I do my best to blunt those temptations, not always perfectly.

I was a pastor for 28 years at a medium sized church in the suburbs of Birmingham, Alabama. Birmingham is a super-spreader of evangelical churches, a veritable canyon of massive gatherings of churchgoing folk. Its similarity to the intensity of football fanaticism has been much observed. But I try to remember that amid the follies of professional religionists, the people in their midst are the same as people everywhere, struggling to raise children, suffering in the midst of life, seeking a connection with the Holy, and yearning for the consolations of authentic faith amid life and death. This is what brings gratitude and joy among us who chose this vocation.

This collection was written during the last year of my full-time pastoral ministry. Writing and music have always been my go-to outlets. It was a place where I could be honest with myself or at least with a bit less editing from the left brain and my acidic self-critic. And this kind of writing also does not always fit within the duties of a pastor. Nevertheless, these personal musings are suffused with faith and doubt and all the things that are the substance of a spiritual life.

That these writings, other than the prayers, were not created with any purpose except to try to pull out and voice what was going on at the time means that they are very personal. The prayers, of course, were given during worship services and reflect more intentional expressions of the moments we shared.

This collection is the second volume that I have done in this style. My earlier book, **Poems Prayers and Unfinished Promises**, was a collection of writings like this, compiled over the period of a church year from the beginning of Advent through Holy Week. This volume begins with Lent of 2020, a time when the global crisis of the pandemic made Lent a truly relevant spiritual exercise on an existential level. Therefore, I thought the two volumes might make interesting companions through an entire devotional year.

In the ancient church, the structuring of a year was a means of instruction in the faith. Each year, the liturgical calendar moves through the biblical story and in particular the Jesus story. In this way, time was defined by the spiritual convictions of the Christian church rather than secular time. Our present day features a 24-hour news cycle, stores and virtual shopping that never end, and the near complete loss of the rhythms of Sabbath and work and prayer. Before we pronounce ourselves progressive in comparison to ancient people, it might do well to revisit their structuring of time.

When I do pastoral prayer, I always think back to something that a Calvinist minister acquaintance said in a presentation I heard thirty-five years ago. He said that in his tradition it was common, unlike more priestly expressions of Christianity, for the minister to stand with his back to God and declare God's word, often accompanied by an accusing finger at the sinners in front of him. But as he gained experience and maturity, he began to imagine himself more and more as he prayed in corporate worship standing like Moses before God with his back to the people, voicing their heartaches and failures and dreams to God.

Like Moses, a good pastor loves his or her people even as there is perpetual disappointment in working with human beings. In public prayer, if it is not to be an exercise of stealth preaching or self-lauding, the minister attempts to be the advocate of the church trying to give voice to what he or she feels and hears and experiences that week among the people God has honored him or her to serve.

Only pastors who listen to their congregation and to the world and its pain can give a pastoral prayer that has a chance to be authentic. It is not primarily about one's artistry or performance. It is more of a corporate confession and requests that one person gives for the sake of others. That is a lofty standard to live up to, and I make no pretense that I have, but I try. It starts with remembering the conversations of people in pain, joy, and struggle during that week.

As for my poems, they come from that deep dark unconscious place somewhere down in my soul where all sorts of things lurk and only stick their heads above water now and then where I can at least partially describe them. I hope you like them, but when I write them, I am not thinking about who might read them or how good they are. They come more as outbursts of words that I cannot quite put into left brain thoughts. And since I am a musician, I tend to find all sorts of little drumming rhythms and melodic turns bursting forth. I love words and so the poems and songs are my attempt to, as Flannery O'Connor once put it, be able to know what I think about something. Until I write it, I don't know what I think.

So, in this little volume if there is something you like, that will make me happy. If you do not like one, you're welcome to go on to the next one. That is the advantage of short writings. My songs are more intentional things since they were written with music I have composed, and I have made that available elsewhere and performed it in front of people. It is hard to give the full effect of a song without the companion tone that the music illustrates, but since they are part poetry and part music, the words can still be useful to read.

I have organized the chapters by eight sections of the liturgical year. Because these writings chronologically began with Lent, I simply chose to begin there, but the book goes through an entire year. Each chapter begins with a pair of haiku that I wrote during the midst of 2020. Otherwise, the book is chronologically organized. Therefore, I warn the reader not to worry too much about structure. Just wander through these woods on a path that meanders back and forth and find whatever might be interesting to you. It's easy enough to pick up and read any place instead of plowing from front to back.

The prayers I included here I share with great trepidation. The very act of sharing a prayer you have written subjects you to the possible charge of audacity and arrogance. But since the very act of praying is unavoidably audacious, I will take my chances. I only hope it might give voice to something that is useful to you or that you recognize in your own experience.

I admire great poets, songwriters, and preachers, and have been influenced by many of them. I learn from them all, but no mentor, teacher or influencer is responsible for this content. But I am grateful for all who gave me words to consider, from parents to teachers to the people I have met, read, studied under, or listened to.

I dedicate this book to my grandchildren, Georgia, Eva Kate, Zadie, and Wallena. At the time that I write this they are the delight of my life and are all children enough still to have retained the joy of play and imagination. It is to them and their future that this volume is lovingly dedicated.

Lent

Lent is a time of special preparation before Easter. The focus has often been on the cross, sacrifice and renunciation. In the ancient church, Lent was often a time in which those excommunicated from the church worked their way through a series of exercises to demonstrate their sorrow and repentance, leading to restoration to membership again if all went well.

However, Lent also was a period (40 days, to coincide with the 40 days Jesus and Moses spent in the wilderness) of testing, sifting, preparation and readiness. Candidates in the ancient church, at the end of lengthy instruction in the faith, made their final preparations during Lent for their baptism on Easter Sunday.

The traditional somber reflection on our sins has its rightful place in the Lenten season. During persecution, it was a time to prepare for the possibility of imminent death.

Transmission

Carrying virus,
sharing death without knowing,
The Fall incarnate.

Blurred Lines

Working now from home
Go to work when I wake up,
Don't know when to stop.

March 2020 Timeline

March 11: The World Health Organization declares the novel coronavirus a pandemic.

> • Actor Tom Hanks and his wife, Rita Wilson, say they've tested positive for the virus.

> • The NBA suspends its season. Most college and pro leagues follow suit. A dozen states close schools. Many people begin working from home. American life grinds to a halt.

March 12: Anthony S. Fauci, the nation's top infectious-disease expert, testifies before Congress that the U.S. testing system is not working. "Yeah, it is a failing," he says. "Let's admit it."

March 13: President Donald Trump declares a national emergency.

March 15: The Centers for Disease Control and Prevention says Americans should cancel gatherings of 50 or more people for two months. Several states impose shutdown orders.

March 16: President Trump tells Americans to avoid gathering in groups of more than 10 and to stop eating in restaurants and taking nonessential trips for the next 15 days. It is the closest the federal government will come to calling for a nationwide shutdown.

March 17: The official U.S. death toll surpasses 100 — and experts predict it will rise quickly.

March 19: President Trump tells Post associate editor Bob Woodward that he has intentionally ... minimized the danger: "I wanted to always play it down. I still like playing it down, because I don't want to create a panic," as Woodward recounts later in his September book.

But it is everywhere. The virus tears through the Seattle region. It's taking hold in New York City — and in Detroit, Chicago, and New Orleans. More than 16,000 people are infected.

March 21: Nursing homes are the first hot spots. Residents account for at least a quarter of all deaths, and probably more. Once inside, the virus is "an almost perfect killing machine."

March 23: Under pressure from conservatives, Trump says he's considering nixing the guidelines for social distancing he announced a week earlier, saying: "We cannot let the cure be worse than the problem itself."

March 26: The United States records its 1,000th official coronavirus death, fewer than 10 days after the toll passed 100. Behind every reported death, every data point on a curve or chart, is a name and a story.

March 28: Trouble with the national stockpile of emergency medical equipment emerges. State and hospital leaders are unable to secure enough masks, ventilators, and other essential gear.

The Gift of Life
February 2020

As the anxiety over the Covid-19 virus stirred into our consciousness, I sent this prayer to friends who were dealing with death—a friend whose beloved wife had died, another whose child died unexpectedly.

A Prayer for Friends Who Have Lost Loved Ones

Life in its beginning, life at the end,
all is pure and true gift
beautiful and real.

That there can be life at all, pulsing, real,
changing us by holding onto it, astounds.

Love is real. It dents our cynicism and pride,
changes us, and breaks our hearts when we let it in.

Hope is so fragile in this world amid the darkness and suffering all around us,
but it is real.

It dares us to lift our eyes from anger and despair
to believe that it all means something.

Faith, so powerful when we first meet it, is tested, and tested again, beaten down, battered by the relentlessness of injustice in the world.

And yet faith circles back and keeps whispering
"Trust, believe, hold on."

It is so real, even against the disappointments of life that do not work out
    and journeys cut short or filled with suffering and pain.

This gift, our lives, the lives that touch us,
they ask us to hold our faith, hope and love,
though the pain mocks us,
    but we do hold on.

It is a mystery, O God, that the treasures we are given are so quickly gone
    yet in our memory they are eternal and so real.
    They point us to You.

Remembering deepens our hope, strengthens our faith, multiplies our love,
even as it causes us to ache all day long with pain and suffering,

As it did and does mysteriously for Thee.

And so, we continue to pray
in Jesus' name who took upon Himself a suffering world

As an act of divine love. Amen.

The Storm Begins
March 2020

As February headed to a close, I had completed the last of several meetings to roll out a series of presentations of a new app and website for a not-for-profit I helped found, the Alabama Coalition for Healthy Mothers and Children. The project was picking up speed as we sought to list faith organizations and helping agencies and services in our state to give away to the public. I was busy with this project, as well as with my church work.

At church, we were in one of our endless promotional times to encourage participation. As I anticipated winding up my final year, I hoped to go out on a high note. Maybe we did, but not the one I imagined. For the past few years, we had planned on a churchwide retreat, alternating between going away to a setting nearby with having a "day apart" on the church grounds. The aim was to facilitate more time together as members.

In our newsletter, I supplied the reasons for members to attend. In that piece, I wrote that

> koine is the New Testament word for "fellowship." But it is deeper. It means "in common." We have Christ in common, but we discover that there is so much more than we thought when we "spend time" in each other's company…It is a day of relationship building. It's a great day as a newcomer or visitor to get to know some of the people who come to church with you.

Little did we know that we would long for the chance to sit together, for the simple pleasure of seeing human faces, talking together, and eating together. About that same time my wife, Vickie, began to say as we watched the news of the strange virus in China and Europe that she was worried. As usual, she was right. She had begun stocking up, and especially was concerned about our daughter who lived in New York City. She asked me to send her a list of items to stock up on. I sent this on February 28 to our children.

Clorox wipes and cleaning supplies
Masks and gloves
Cereal and almond milk u don't have to refrigerate.
Cans of tuna, black beans, rice, canned food.

That email would prove prophetic.

Ash Wednesday, in an odd bit of timing, was on February 26. It was the last time our church would celebrate communion together for most of the year of 2020. Ash Wednesday marks a 40-day remembrance of Jesus' forty days and nights in the desert wilderness, tempted by the devil as he considered his calling. According to tradition, this occurred near Jericho, marked today by a perilous monastery on a cliffside, where Jesus would have looked down on the green palms of that city where the rich spent their winters during the dry season, fed by Elisha's spring.

That spot, of course, would make perfect sense for the Satanic temptation to appear in the mind of Jesus. "Just serve me, cut corners, abandon God's calling, and you can have the whole world, all of its riches and prosperity." Jesus, thankfully, refused.

Lent is a Christian time of repentance from our worldliness and sins. Many Christians fast in various ways. Fasting, as my friend Rev. Ron DelBene said to me once, is practicing "non-compulsive attachment" to things of life.

As the United States of America continued to enjoy a roaring economy and faced an election year, we were also mired in a bitter impeachment hearing. Our lack of reconciliation on every hand simmered below surfaces of Wall Street records and outward success. It was an odd juxtaposition of prosperity and struggle. Haves and have nots saw and continued to see a widening gulf between them, thanks to a revolutionary economy driven increasingly away from traditional sources of wealth and into information technology. It exacerbated the sense of being left out for many.

Now into this moment came a tiny, microscopic entity, a virus. Odd, indeed, since phrases like "viral" have invaded our daily language. We speak of a video of some inane action posted online as "going viral," without a thought as to its goodness, moral value, or real importance to life.

Now came a genuine virus. Truthfully in retrospect, its invasion was well underway, but most of the earth didn't realize it yet.

The color displayed during Lent in the liturgical traditions is purple, the color of sorrowful repentance. Repentance is in short supply in a capitalistic and optimistic America. It is endlessly fascinating that we alternate politically from portraying our nation as both falling away from its better times and being the greatest nation in history. But that is what idols do—they obscure the truth.

In fact, America is a wonderful nation, and blessed beyond measure materially, but in that history, there is both darkness and light, sin, and grace. All would be on display in 2020 as we wrestled together, brought to our knees by a tiny microbe that was no respecter of persons. Rich and poor, healthy, and sick, the Covid-19 variant coronavirus sought only for a host to inhabit and move on.

The virus was not itself, of course, the temptation before us. Human history is replete with pandemics and the Christian church and other religions have plenty of historical precedent for ministry in such times. The bubonic plague in medieval Europe, known as the Black Death, killed one third of the continent's population in its time.

The 1918 Flu epidemic killed fifty million people worldwide, and that just following the devastation of World War I. Like the present, people argued and debated about going on with life or sheltering in place. Fateful public health decisions were made that resulted in unnecessary deaths. There are plenty of examples of arguments about masks and other health measures.

No, the temptations facing us, and indeed the world, had to do with our response to this terrible moment. Would we pull together or fall apart? Would we put truth at the forefront or not? Sadly, the answers are not pleasant. Despite extraordinary achievements by pharmaceutical companies, governments, and researchers to fast track the development of a lifesaving array of vaccines for the coronavirus, the next year would also bring a time of blaming, anger, fear, and failure.

Sometimes the season of Lent is not about ultimate victory but perseverance. The Christian story is about an undertaking of the greatest severity on behalf of others by Jesus of Nazareth, an undertaking that He embodied fully in his life, teachings, healings, example, and exorcisms. It is the arduous way, the way of voluntary entry into the lives of others, even to the point of suffering, which is the way of truth.

The failures of 2020 are easier to see now in retrospect. We all failed to live in the readiness required for human life that is always under threat. Prosperity, not hardship, is the true enemy of the spiritual life. Ease of living lulls us to sleep and can tempt us to self-deception.

Perseverance, however, did happen in 2020. Families turned attention toward feeding neighbors, helping one another, and pitching in. Ignorant and angry responses were everywhere to be seen, as were those merchants of blaming and self-serving. But down where pastors usually live, we saw another angle of view. People comforted one another, now on cell phones instead of in person.

Somehow, we carried on, adjusted, changed to meet the moment. The mood of March was filled with fear and the unknown. No one knew for certain how this new threat was transmitted. Despite the instant communication available through the internet, we were humbled by the virus. It would take time. We would walk into stores, not knowing if we would get sick by touching something or breathing next to the wrong person.

We were watching images on the news of massive deaths in Europe and Asia and hoping, absurdly, that we would be spared. We closed our borders, although the virus was already spreading, invisibly and rapidly.

People died in ICUs alone and suffocating, held by gloved hands of weeping nurses and physicians. We headed toward a cataclysm in the public health system from a lack of capacity. Years of failing to prepare for the worst left us scrambling.

As the crisis became nationally named, we shifted into survival mode. Churches faced a terrible dilemma. Our very lives, institutionally, depended on being together, relationships and commitments reinforced by regular and extensive gathering. At the heart of the Baptist vision of church is the gathered local congregation. Every other Christian tradition, whatever their official theology of church, depends on the same.

What would we do if the very act that kept us alive and thriving were suddenly taken away?

Pastoral Prayer
March 1, 2020

God grant that we may
    have the mind of Christ--
He who didn't mind giving up the spotlight,
    whose security was in Your will
and whose perspective was large enough
    To include us all.

Grant us to have the heart of Jesus
who sees possibility under the pain,
and hope amid the ruins of life.

Grant that we might, with Your divine help,
    become Your hands and feet,
Walking down long-forgotten roads
    to find those who live alone and
    those who are forlorn and weighted with sorrow.

Only help us not to be afraid,
    not to shrink and crumble
not to run from the pain that will come by going forward.

Create in us a great energy of community building
in a land where we have inexplicably become weary of one another.
Open our hearts to fellowship and the richness of others
    amid the poverty of soul created by anger and suspicion.
Liberate us from virtual lives on phones and devices, lives made up only of
    images and words and reactions to words
so we may find the living of real lives fed by the Living Word
by whom worlds were made, sinners redeemed, and death overcome.

We can only do it because You first loved us
    and sent Jesus to teach us how to die to those choices
which would kill us eventually anyway.
    He died so we might truly live at last
because You are with us,
        by Your Holy Spirit. Amen.

Blessing
March 10. 2020

On Tuesday, March 10, before the declaration of emergency, I was asked to bring an opening prayer to the Vestavia Hills Chamber of Commerce meeting.

Before the meeting, some older men I was conversing with dismissed the seriousness of the moment. They chuckled when I mentioned my concern. One said, "Preacher, are you scared of this virus?" I said, "I am deeply concerned. And you ought to be. You are in the high-risk group." They looked at me like I had lost my faith. It seemed far from the South, this problem in New York, but many of us were beginning to be alarmed.

Here is the prayer I prayed as the blessing that day. Given at the Chamber of Commerce monthly meeting, Vestavia Hills, Alabama, March 10, 2020,

God of grace and mystery, healing, and love
In this moment, we pray
      For health workers and the CDC, and all in positions of care--
      Protect their lives, use their skills, lift their weariness,
      For lab workers and immunologists, scientists and community leaders,
      Nurses and physicians and those already exposed to illnesses we pray..
      Above all, protect us from fear, hopelessness, and fear of one another.
      I pray that we have courage to pull together, to weather the storm
      to be prudent, to carry on, to trust amid the torrent of
      blame and accusations and anger.
Help us instead to direct our energies to healing
and the desire to protect one another with all our might.
But these are things we pray always.
It is not death we fear
      but hopelessness in facing sickness and death.
Strengthen our faith, our common resolve,
our love for one another and for all of humanity.
We ask that we not shrink back in adversity, but step forward, unafraid,
to continue our caring, fight the good fight, build peace,
      deepen trust and strengthen hope.
Bless this food we share, the work we each do,
and all the families represented here,
parents and children, grandparents and kin
and may we bless one another and all we meet all day long. Amen.

Pastoral Prayer,
Sunday, March 15, 2020

Mighty God,
We come in a time when we feel helpless
until we remember the times when You have worked in an extraordinary way:
    in the history of Israel, in the life of Jesus, in the early church,
        through the great saints of all ages,
in our own lives,
through the people who love, nurtured us, and led us to You.

So, we come today to do what we do every day,
and that is to lift our hearts in praise to You
    and in confident trust to say, "You have the words of life."
We are people who in recent days
have been bombarded by distressing information and news.
You already know where we are.
What we most want is for You to show us Your way through,
    that does not lead us on the path of fear, abandonment,
    and loneliness.

Today we come because our hearts are filled with concern for others.
All of us have people we are worried about
because of their health situations, circumstances, isolation and fear.
We pray for those working morning to night to take care of the sick,
    And for their safety and wellbeing.
We pray for leaders and for the churches everywhere.
Guide us, we pray. In Jesus' name, Amen.

Pastoral Prayer
April 1, 2020

"Your love, O Lord, reaches to the heavens,
      Your faithfulness to the skies.
Your righteousness is like a mighty mountain,
      Your justice like the great deep.
O Lord, You preserve both man and beast.
How priceless is Your unfailing love." (Psalm 36:5-7, NRSV)

Lift up our eyes, O Lord, to see Your light
      when we walk in the midst of darkness.
This present darkness around us seeps into the soul.
When we least expect it, it shrouds our hearts in depression and loss of hope
      it pounds us with statistics and news reports
      it buffets us endlessly with doubts about Your providence.
The darkness seeps with indifference into our hearts--
      it minimizes the agony of suffering and sin
      it shrugs with apathy toward the pain of the world
      the shadows tempt us to stop caring
            and shake the foundations of our hope.

The night hides the efforts of our lives
      we worry that dawn may never come
            that no answers will satisfy, and that greed will always win the day.
Will selfishness always prevail? Is self-giving destined to fail?

Strengthen us for the night, O Lord,
      when our flesh fails, let our spirits find Your might.
Help us never to forget in our strivings
      that with You is the fountain of life,
      and that in Your light we see light.

Illumine our hearts, shed light on our paths
      fill our minds with the brightness of Your word,
      and brighten our homes with radiant love.
Cause our memories to glow with remembrance
      that we would remain faithful in the journey
      and undaunted by the darkness.

Help us recall that the darkness does not comprehend the light--
    the Light is shining in the darkness and always will.
Let our lights so shine, in Jesus' name we pray. Amen.

Pontius Pilate
April 4, 2020

In the Year of Handwashing, 2020
He may be a most fitting saint. Trying to play it safe
and keep Rome's unforgiving eye off of Palestine and himself.
He instead lit the fuse for a faith that swept the world—
Not by accomplishment but by playing to his deepest evasions.
He didn't listen to the warning of his wife.
He caved to the guilt of the mob who tweaked his deepest fears.
He tried to wash his hands of it—
Which insured that we would remember
Forever.

He alone had the power to crucify
He handed Jesus' life over to petty bureaucrats. Why?
Driven by age old feuds and lies
Pilate caved, ensuring that Jesus would die.

Jesus of course said Pilate couldn't take His life from Him.
So Jesus, too, handed His life over—willingly—
to the handwringers and pious hand scrubbers,

But the virus that kills cannot be scrubbed off so easily
And it was set loose on the world
simultaneously with a remedy.
Washing hands is a stopgap, but
no substitute
for vaccination or actual truth.

Atticus
April 4, 2020

Atticus Finch we could use you now
you didn't flinch, no man, no how,
But if Miss Lee's other view
About coming of age is true,
the lionized courage the little girl saw
came in your one moment's cause.
The truth that such can come from us
(who are nine parts water and one of dust),
Makes the moment the lion fights
More amazing in second light.

Atticus, however flawed you be,
Nevertheless, the little child's hero we want to see
we could use you while viewing cowardice
and each day's spineless sycophants--

That with the millions on the line,
sparks of you will somehow find
their moment here and there in each
where both of you urge us to speak.

.

Webinarious
April 4, 2020

The plague, perhaps a virus from some bat,
launches from some filthy marketplace,
And from that one dirty rat
Now homemade masks cover all our faces.

Wash your hands, don't kiss, don't hug
But far worse than imprisonment
or going out in rubber gloves
Is all the virtual help I'm drowning in.

The cause of this, in a biblical view
Is that we who were cursed in Genesis
To keep cash moving from me to you,
Guaranteed work became our thorny nemesis.

And I'm fairly certain a line can be traced
From then to now in the human race.
While stuck at home, both near and far,
to drown in required webinars.

Holy Week

Holy Week is that time when Christians all over the world remember the final week of Jesus' life. It begins with Palm Sunday, when the crowds welcomed Jesus into the city where he would die five days later.

The center of Holy Week is the Cross and its pinnacle is the empty tomb on Easter morning, when Christ was raised from the dead by God. This Passion story--Jesus' life, death and resurrection--was the heart of the early church's proclamation. Small in number, facing hostility in their world, the church clung to their simple and life-changing story: No matter how messed up the world, Someone had come to make a difference. Jesus' death overpowered the darkness of sin. Jesus' resurrected life was God's defeat of the ultimate power of death. Holy Thursday, or "Maundy Thursday" marks the evening when Jesus took the Passover meal with his disciples and instituted what we call "communion" or the "Lord's Supper." "Maundy Thursday" comes from the Latin, "Mandatum Novum" ("new commandment") for the new commandment that Jesus gave to his disciples, that we love one another. Good Friday is a service marking the crucifixion. It is a somber remembrance of Jesus' death on the cross.

Erosion

One day vanishes
into the next without a
signpost--hopes weaken

On a Vent

Dying all alone
Amid caring strangers here,
wearing masks and gloves.

Living and Dying Alone

My last year of fulltime pastoral ministry forced us to profoundly deviate from some of the most time-honored behaviors of our usual routine and education. I was trained to be with people. I doubt there was a week during the first forty years of pastoral ministry that I did not visit a hospital, a nursing home, someone's home, or have coffee or lunch with a member. Not to mention hours of conversations in incidental moments—hearing about a heartache in the grocery store, aisle 4 when you bump into a member.

Pastoral work depends not only on the scheduled places of connection like worship and preaching and teaching but, like Jesus taught us, going wherever people are and always being ready to listen and speak a word of the gospel hope. I have counseled marriages in the bleachers at ballgames, listened to terrible childhoods while riding to a meeting and heard confessions in the parking lot of Walmart.

One day, not too long before the pandemic, I drove to University Hospital to see a member before surgery. Three family members were there in the crowded waiting room, and we laughed and bantered but also had important conversation about what their loved one was facing. As I got up to leave, a woman in a family sitting across from us leaned forward and touched my arm. "Are you a pastor?"

"Yes, ma'am."

"I wonder if you'd pray for my mother." And she went on to tell me about the situation. They were from another town, alone with this. I sat down and heard the story and said, "Why don't we pray for her right here?"

This has happened often through the years. At funerals, weddings, all of the turning points of life, you are there as a representative of something bigger and more important than you yourself. If you handle it well, people are drawn to you. You learn not to be irritated by the interruptions of the "important things" You think you should be doing. Eventually I determined that these interruptions were about as close to Jesus as I'd ever be and stopped being frustrated about them. When a woman reaches through a crowd to touch you, you learn to pick it up. Something important is here.

And so, along with preaching alone, I found myself in 2020 being a pastor without crowds and visits and the constant, beautiful interruptions. If we were together, we were told, we might spread the Death slithering in our midst.

And yet, there is this unavoidable truth about calling to ministry—you are called to be there, with them, in the extreme places of their lives. Truthfully, I miss this aspect of my vocation the most. Upon retirement this void was more pronounced, but during the Last Year, this was an intrusion of an unnatural governor on the engine of our work. We had to resort to the phones, emails, video and Facetime (more than once I called someone and talked with them on an iPhone with my iPad so I could see their face as we talked). We asked the staff to call repeatedly to check in with members. It is the lifeblood of church, and to forsake it is to abandon the calling altogether.

Unfortunately, nursing homes and hospitals shut down. Only one family member, and usually only at the point of possible death, could come in during a hospital stay. It was the right call, but suddenly people who were already isolated and depressed by sickness and the prospect of death were also cut off from the very support they needed. Of the half million people who died of Covid during the Last Year, many had only a screen visual contact, or a phone or perhaps only the hand of a nurse while they breathed their last. It was a horrible end of life.

Those in nursing facilities and assisted living, meanwhile, sat in deep isolation to protect them. That same isolation assaulted their health in another way—the loss of social and familial presence. The news was full of stories of loved ones driving past and waving at a window for just a glimpse of someone they loved. It was a dark valley through which we passed.

As the year rolled on, of course, certain realities had to be faced and innovative and often odd ways of carrying on conjured up. For a while, our committee watching over the health of the congregation restricted our gatherings to ten or less. For quite a while, then, when a death occurred, we had to face the painful reality that a person whose life had touched so many others could not have opportunity for gathering all those, not even counting family members, who normally would come and embrace one another.

Funerals in the South particularly are social events. There is healing in funeral rituals in all cultures, and what is universal is the "coming together." People eat, laugh, cry, and tell stories that buoy up the family. It is a hard time as it is, but without these consolations and connections, the emptiness and incompleteness are amplified.

How achingly hard it is not to come and embrace our friends. This pandemic robbed us even of the comforts we might give the dying and one another. It is as though a great wave of heartache had swept over the entire planet.

Our church staff, like those in all congregations and organizations, had to ask, "How will we do this now that we cannot do it as we once did?" "Touch," connection, and being together are so crucial to the existence of any organization, but there are peculiar ways that we do church. Communion, literally "in common" is ideally done with shared loaf and common cup. But we had to offer our first "virtual" Maundy Thursday and Easter, too.

How would we ordain without the laying on of hands? How could we have Sunday School for children and classes for older adults without being in the building? Should we take temperatures and administer tests before baptism? A lot to think about.

This is not without precedent, of course. The church has been through all sorts of times in history when gathering was difficult or even temporarily impossible. And innovation always resulted from such times. These become the new "rituals." Ritual is necessary. It is the way we negotiate passages in life. So, we had to reinvent them. Rituals are the markers for the "rhythms" of life. You can't work all the time, play all the time, or heaven forbid, be online all the time. You have to do other things. Some patterns carried on, but others had to be reconceived.

I did my first online memorial service for Dr. William Poe. The only live event was the graveside service in Tuscaloosa with eight of us present--three caregivers, his son Allan and daughter Jody, Cherri Morriss and two funeral directors. It was a beautiful day and we stood round the outside of the green awning over the grave. Everyone was masked except me. *The Lord's Prayer* by Malotte and *Amazing Grace* were sung acapella. I read a selection from a little book Dr. Poe had written, a memoir. The chapter I read was about the faithfulness of God in all things. Dr. Poe, a historian, missionary and professor, had met with me a few years earlier and planned an elaborate funeral. I hope he smiled at the irony in heaven.

It was different, but in other ways, it was the same—we prayed, we worshiped, we remembered. And there was the familiar solemnity that is inevitable at a graveside. We had finished a responsibility to one another, passed through the door from one part of life to another, and turned to the new time.

What we discovered in this odd time when our love had to be imagined and transmitted through symbols across screens is that certain realities abide. Relationship endures. That we had fellowship before the Great Separation enabled us not to completely be separated emotionally and spiritually, only physically.

I have marveled at the innovations of my fellow staff members as they have labored creatively to keep the church together, moving and continuing its life. I appreciated the extraordinary and manifold giftedness of the people of Vestavia Hills Baptist Church and its members in adapting. I don't know what "the new normal" will be down the road, but the essential realities of our life in this world carried on just fine.

We could not hug, shake hands, or eat together, but love still connected us, unstoppably. We still did the things we needed to do, and God showed us new ways that still accomplished it. Even death does not disrupt this extraordinary phenomenon among human beings and God.

What matters is that we do not leave the important work of life undone while waiting for things to work out. That is the great mistake we might make, crisis or no. Life is always here to be lived, the life we have now. The work doesn't change, only figuring out how to get it done varies.

We will and must eventually gather again. Otherwise, we will only have the truncated and pale imitation of life that virtuality affords. From online dating to church, something in us requires an eventual meeting, flesh with flesh, incarnate and real.

The funerals of my final year were unlike any of my entire ministry. I was at risk multiple times, reliant only on a cloth mask to protect me because the scientists racing to produce a vaccine could only go so fast. More than once, I went into rooms full of people to pray, occasionally even to embrace. More than once funerals became the origins of the spread of the disease. There was no way to be church without risk.

Faces
April 5, 2020

Open eyed spark on the day of Your birth
instantly transformed waiting and hurt
into admiration and joy at the sight of baby You.

A face is the strangest creation I've pondered
Two eyes with eyebrows of variable widths
One nose for breathing, a mouth talks and eats
Two ears for hearing, a chin to stroke pensively....

There are 43 muscles in the face,
most are operated by the seventh cranial nerve
that leaves Your skull just in front of Your ears
To do all the work
Smiling, frowning, raging and sad,

A face is a soul that slips outside to be seen—
Causes men to live for one woman's smile,
The eyes tell stories with scarcely a word,
and deep lines remember pain undeserved.
Faces kept in a daddy's wallet or on a screen
        stay close where they can be seen.
But you can't make them to tell a lie--
You can't plaster them over or hide the truth.

Eager children's faces on the first day of school
Barely conceal excitement and fears
Except for the one who adopts a façade
And pretends their boredom with it all.

An earth full of faces of everything—
Laughter and songs and pain and despair
They light up in recognition of someone they know
And love lifts the eyes and turns the corners up

A face, that's the thing that the wardens hide
Put 'em in darkness alone to die.
Just another human face they crave to see
when the light returns temporarily.

When a woman on the street or
in the shelter goes home,
They see her face before she reaches the door.
Eyes are windows that peek into souls,
But they only stir the longing to see more.

That's the hardship of hiding from view
Faces meant to display me for you.
You don't need a mask to hide the real you,
But it makes the job easier,
And it will do.

Coming Through
Song lyric, April 6, 2020 (BMI)

Long black train full of hobos coming from a distant town
They get off here and beg for help with their heads hung down
Angel on fire with a chainsaw breaking in the nursing home
Doctor never saw him go by, she was talking on the phone
But he was coming on through. Nothing she could do

Heavy breathing and tea leaves cleaving to the refugees
Bulletproof babies in chain link cages look out at me.
Watch the screen while leaning towers come crashing down
Pale horse rider gallops past the biggest house in town.
Just coming through, no matter what we do.

Rotten smell from people not well in the air outside
Old people choking and young people smoking, and they turn a blind eye.
The emperor's clothes burned up in the dumpster fire
Smoke is rising and the sirens racing to the funeral pyre
Watch out, they're coming through! No matter what we do.

Everybody wants to know the reason why
Pointing at each another, looking at the sky
Still coming through.

Preacher down in Texas says the Judgement Day is coming on
The wrath is coming he said from his hundred-million-dollar throne
He's got the Good Book rolled up in his hand
But he's the royal jester, he doesn't understand
What's really coming through, no matter what they do.

I saw a dimly burning wick that somehow doesn't die
A hero in the slaughterhouse who somehow stays alive
Rises from the shadows that still linger here,
A beam of light pierces through the deepest fear,
And it's coming through. No matter what I do.
It's coming through for me and you.

Holy Week always calls up memories of four trips I've made to Israel. I never seem to exhaust what I find there. This was a memory from 2010 that came up.

Walking Around Jerusalem
April 9, 2020

Up before dawn by the New Gate
On the day we planned to go home
I got the notion to walk around the Old City
And set out alone.

I'd come as a picture-snapping tourist years before
To run where Jesus walked on ancient cobblestones.
This time, I came as pilgrim
to listen and sing with the adoring throngs.

I made my way along capricious, sloping hills
Pink dawn gleamed overhead
But I lost the path and wound up
In some backyard instead.

Contemplation dissolved
in the cold sweat of lostness.
How could simple circumference
Twist into a knot and dead end?

Without any point of reference,
No choice but soldier on with shallow breaths of fear
    I heard only Hebrew and Arabic--
    I was the stranger here.

At last! a noisy street, and merchants
setting fruit and bread outside
Setting up their storefronts with
Cars and buses moving by.

Each section of the journey
A world unto itself
I kept scanning the horizon
for the familiar door from which I left.

I came at last to see it
And walked back just in time
To see my fellow pilgrims
In the breakfast line.

I'd walked around the city
It took an hour or more
I was vulnerable and foolish
When I went out the door.

I was glad that I came back
With nothing to report
Except that I had done it
And it took an hour or more.

Not a single bomb or terrorist
No kidnapping or guns
To live up to my expectations
of the way this place was run.

Good Friday
April 10, 2020

Morning coffee comes to our cells,
We are not in jail, we are monks of the pandemic
"Go to your cell. It will teach you everything."
This time can teach us, too.
We can go to Good Friday here.

By three o'clock, the world shaken,
The darkness a shadow across our souls,
the failures and oblivion of us all fully revealed
      and judged.
By three o'clock, the thieves will have died, too.
The crowd dispersed, the disciples disheartened,
His mother and the Beloved Disciple,
Having to keep their distance, wait to receive His body.
All will descend into silence.

Even Easter will begin with a graveyard disruption
A woman alone
And disciples hiding behind locked doors.

We can do this.

Preaching Alone
April 11, 2020

The camera and lights are set up, and the cameraman
Lifts an index finger and lets it fall to the side. "Action."
I walk up to the pulpit, just like real lift, and open my Bible
I take off my mask, look into the camera, and pretend to see them.
After all these years I know their faces and locations.
Despite all the useless complaints about people sitting in "their pew,"
Human beings covet a place that is theirs,
To see familiar places, to worship in familiar ways,
To cry, be comforted, laugh, and pray.

Now it is all imagination. I learn to do it.
But it is only the hope of seeing them again, gathered,
Calling name after name every Sunday,
That keeps me going.

As pandemic rages, they are huddled at home or the lake
Or alone, staring at me on a screen.
"In that day even the Introverts will long
To see another human being."
Well, maybe so.

I see a picture on Facebook from Christmas
Orchestra, choirs, and a packed church.
I remember children running through the halls
And being spontaneously hugged by a seven-year-old.
The joy of remembering triggers loss.
"If I forget You, O Jerusalem…."

Easter

Easter was originally called Pascha by the early church, a word derived from the Hebrew meaning "passover." "Later it became known as "Easter," from the Anglo-Saxon spring goddess, Eostre, whose festival occurred during the spring equinox. The filter through which the early church understood the story of Jesus was resurrection. The early Christians were convinced that Jesus of Nazareth, who was crucified by the Romans, had been raised to life by God. The entire story of Jesus, then, is understandable only in reverse. By viewing it through the conviction born on Easter, we understand the whole meaning of his life, his teachings, and even his death.

Change

Thrown out of routine
The crisis awakens us
To innovations.

Walking

It has been so long
since I cherished trees and birds
And moved so slowly

Pastoral Prayer, Easter Sunday
April 8, 2020

Everlasting Lord,
This Easter Sunday our imaginations race to the tomb.
We have been artificially stopped in our tracks.
    No longer driven and racing from event to event
    No complaining about too much to do or juggling multiple demands.
We're working as hard as ever, but mostly in solitude
and in our heads and on screens.
We have never had busier times, and we have never been more alone
    But we have also never worshipped You more greedily.

At the mouth of the tomb that first Easter, just before He was revealed,
    I imagine a great silence—full of sadness, heartache, lostness
    as Mary and her companions trudged along
to do the unpleasant duties of mourning.
There is silence, and then… all is new.

It is the same silence of deep prayer,
the silence of a knowing glance between old friends
who can speak a hundred words with a smile and twinkling eyes.

This Easter, Vatican square is empty of people.
The Pope lifts empty hands, alone.
Churches are filled with memories but not bodies
Homes are filled with anxiety and leaning forward
But not the noise of the whole family gathered.

Still, there are gifts in this Easter silence
Our sense of what matters is challenged and changed.
    We are traveling lighter,
    We are full of new visions and cooperative spirit
We are tossing artificial barriers to the side
    Streamlining all that is unnecessary for the moment.
In this silence we walk to the tomb,
And ask that You fill us with an ever-deeper awe
when we again return to our places of worship.

We confess that, like the disciples that Easter morning,
> our expectations are muddled and fearful,
>> but we want to be confronted by You.

Give us courage to worship in spirit and truth where we are.
> Hold us together,
> Join our hearts,
>> and, having heard You, to obey You in our lives.

As we create new organization and new plans,
> Raise us up first with Christ himself, to live as resurrection people,
>> To rebuild our lines of communication spiritually with You
>>> And to move to new levels of faithfulness.

This is a new day, and it is Your work among us.
As we come today to give to the birthing of a new era in Your church,
> Multiply our gifts and time and spirit
>> That they may glorify You mightily in the years ahead.
>> In Jesus' name. Amen.

Thunderstorm
April 19, 2020

"Funder," is what our babies called it
Before their little tongues could make a "th" sound.
"I don't like funder."
I understand—it comes up from underneath even
as it rolls across the sky, a preview of Second Coming,
Especially close-up and right behind flashing sheets of light.

As I get older, and my body denies my denials
I am learning to sit inside,
looking out at thick walls of lush Alabama trees.
The rumble is backdrop.

I also see the oak trees, relieved to be shed of humans for a while,
The rain finds every leaf and gives it a drink,
Not knocking them off this time, just a gentle tap,
And each leaf in syncopated time
quickly bends down and springs back up,
Eager to catch the next drop.

Having clicked off the television blaring bad news
There is only green peace and quiet that taps the eyes and ears
And gives my senses a drink, too.
For a moment, nothing costs anything but my attention.

Authority
April 19, 2020

"All authority on heaven and earth has been given me."
Words as terrifying as an empty tomb without explanation.
Confusing stories about Your appearances
And passing through locked doors.
The things You are telling us now in the light of Easter
Send shivers of disorientation through us.
If you quit yielding to the powers turned upside down
all that we know and trust,
What then?

Lost
April 19, 2020

This is about all I've learned
in six decades of guiding others
through thick woods of thorns
and uncertain footing:

You seek, but do not find
until you first account for what you've lost.
For grief is the measure of
love's most bittersweet cost.

Suffering is the plumb line
of all that matters most.
Problem solving is no comfort
when you walk among the ghosts.

You must stop to take account
of the empty space—there is no hurrying.
That is the part of moving through
I find most maddening

It is so intensely unpleasant
that you'd as soon run through,
but it makes it stretch out longer
No matter what you do.

Look carefully where you step—
walk a measured pace instead.
Pay attention
until you reach a clearing up ahead.

Pastoral Prayer,
Youth Sunday, April 20, 2020

Loving God,
In this time above all others
we are prone to impatience, anger and frustration—
routines of family, friendships and leisure have been blown apart.
We are scrambling to get through each day.
Remind us, Lord--
we are still raising the children of our villages
and launching them into life--
even this life.

We forget too quickly that to live is to grow and learn and change and adapt.
At times we want to scream, but then we remember
earlier generations who passed through pandemics and shutdowns,
Wars and depressions,
massive changes beyond the reach of any one of us.
If our instant access to media fools us into thinking otherwise,
the truth is, we are quieted down into sacrifice, discipline, patience, and hope.
We have suddenly fast forwarded from boom to bust,
from thriving to living on the fly.

Help us, like Jesus, to see the possibilities in this moment,
Not the ones we wish for or think ought to be.
And to remember, we are always modeling, teaching, learning.
Contentment is a powerful weapon in this war.
We would learn to be happy without the normal rituals of our lives
And have the few that are available,
To live in a rhythm that remembers that each day is still a treasure to be found.
We pray for our youth and children
That as they, too, are negotiating changed expectations and routines
That there is something for them to see and learn
That they will be resilient when this storm passes--
Mindful of its lessons, and changed into more mature faith by it.

On this day, we recognize their gifts,
acknowledge their aspirations, bless their efforts, and hear their questions.
> Help us not to stand in their way, but without abandoning them.

Teach us how to affirm them
without abdicating our responsibility to discipline and protect them.
Help us to be quick to bless, slow to criticize and ready to understand.
May our correction be always done in a spirit that invites them
toward responsibility and maturity.

For all the children and youth of the world we pray—
That they might know the full and abundant life that You wish to give us all.
Help us to work with all our might for that life to be true for all:
> To care more deeply for Your kingdom than our own desires
> > To work for justice more than to strive for our own place in the sun.
> > To seek the truth above the temptation to rationalize.

We are most thankful for Christian community and for this fellowship.
May our children remember always what we taught them,
May they never forget that
here they were told the story of Jesus and his grace.
May they always know this as a community
that sees You at work in their lives
and calls them out to follow You.
In Jesus' name. Amen.

Poor Virus
April 26, 2020

Imagine!
Everywhere you go, even though you affect everyone around you,
billions of people fear you, and everyone knows your name.
The whole world hates you and wants you to die.

It's not like you had a great childhood—born of a bat-bite
In a filthy wet market. Or did you flee on a lab worker's breath?
You were bound to be wild.

You make people sick.
Your existence is one relationship to the next,
But everything you touch gets sick or dies.

Mercifully, you don't have a heart, a brain,
feelings, sensitivity or the need to be loved.
A bit of genetic goop is all You are,
moving from one to the next.
Fever-giving, life sucking, lung-clogging little covid—
Just go away already.

Pastoral Prayer
May 6, 2020

Even when the quarantine is lifted, we discover a place of being alone.
It goes with us. In the boat, to the beach or the mountains,
A moment in the day when the shadow pierces our good cheer
and that place of the long loneliness rises up to look at us,
threatening our well-being.

We must learn how to pray here. It asks us to have courage,
Because we don't always know if what we're asking
is the right thing at all.

We are shooting in the dark here, grabbing at straws.
Truth is hard to come by.
We're more or less defined by who we listen to,
what we chose to read, who we believe
And who we write off before we even hear what they have to say.

And then we come here into Your presence, Eternal God,
and our hearts melt before You,
because You know what we don't.
and You know what only You and I know and no one else does.
and You know that in our choosing and living
we are like children walking next to a steep cliff,
oblivious to the choices we make without thinking.

We don't really know how it will all work out.
and we don't know if the path we are on will let us all live out the year.
It's that kind of moment.

But we know this: that we are here, now, today, in this moment with You.
We know that Jesus called us His friend, and He is faithful.
We know that we have others in our lives to cherish and who cherish us.

On this day, when normally we are fussing with graduation plans
and mother's gifts and lunch plans,
We are tender in heart, less certain than usual,
rattled in confidence and concerned about tomorrow.

We are worried about people we love, sad with separations,
and bored out of our minds with sheltering

Yet there are many gifts coming to us afresh—
gifts of kindness and neighbor concern.
We cherish our congregation with fresh intensity.
What is taken away is suddenly seen clearly.
We long to gather again, sing with one voice,
hail one another with smiles and greetings.
Today we ask for freedom of heart and mind,
freedom to be content within,
freedom of trust for our needs,
freedom to love and freedom to care and help.
Freedom from anxious fear of one another, freedom from the fear of dying.

On this day we pray for every family and every home in the world
For mothers whose hearts ache with separation from their children
Or saddened by the changes in their children's lives.
For families worrying about paying bills and making ends meet,
Juggling school and learning to do basic things in new ways.
For graduates and their loved ones
whose celebrations are stunted and delayed.
For expectant mothers anxious about the uncertainty of the world
       their baby is coming into
For mothers and families whose hopes are shaking.
For children frightened of a world suddenly veering
into a place they do not understand.
Give us faith that is real
Hope that is durable
And love that is sure.
And make of us all people whose treasures are not only in this world,
Lest when earthly treasure are lost, we will not be. Through Christ our Lord.
Amen.

Untold Tales from the Exile
May 13, 2020

We heard from Jeremiah
Ezekiel and all the rest
about Bubonic Babylonians
come to tear apart the nest.

They marched the poor Judeans
into exile to be stuck--
but were there smaller stories
that never made the final cut.

Did they form support groups
like "Babylonian 101?"
Did parents tell kids stories
about the old folks back home?

Did their children stomp, refuse to go
when Cyrus sent them home,
because they wished to graduate
with their friends in Babylon?

Was there graffiti on the hallowed
Hanging Garden walls that said
"Nabonidus is a doo-doo brain"
and "Marduk is dead"?

Were there articles in *Exile Daily*
to help the refugees
adjust to the new normal
of life as minority?

These are the stories I'd like to find,
but they're probably hid from view
swept away by history
as my poetry will be, too.

Pastoral Prayer
Memorial Day, Sunday, May 29, 1994

Mighty God,
We come today to pray for our families.
We are filled with thanksgiving for the family that formed us
    Fed and clothed and read to us,
        Sought our opportunities for us when we could not choose.
We celebrate the joys and pleasures of our homes
    as well as acknowledge honestly the difficulties
        of meshing our personalities and contradictions
    with our obligations.
Broken families that embody all the contradictions and failures of our world
Families where violence and violation are the rule
and rules do not exist as well as those where rules and expectations are so many and so harsh as to squelch life itself.
Homes where love has long departed,
leaving only sad memories and unfulfilled longings
We also come on this Memorial Day to think tenderly of mothers and fathers
who sent their sons and daughters out
to those desolate places
where the world's violence had erupted into war.

Their children never came home.
We thank You for the lives of the dead, whose gift
reminds us of both the preciousness of life
and the costly fragility of liberty.

Remind us, as well, of our family responsibilities,
for our spouses whom You have given us to love
    and our children, whom You have entrusted to our care.
Make our homes spiritual centers
        where Your divine calling is sought
        Your holy voice is revered
        and Your Spirit's gifts are recognized in one another,
    Far above the clamor of the world and the television.

Thank You, too, for the family of God,
that great family that has a place at Your table for every child,
where every believer is our kin,
and every child an heir of its riches.
Let us seek always to enlarge Your family by welcoming others
and enrich Your family by the willing gift of our lives to its upbuilding.

Through Jesus our Lord. Amen.

Pentecost

Pentecost comes fifty days after Passover in the Hebrew calendar ("Pente" meaning "fifty"). It was a festival in ancient Israel when pilgrims came to the city to commemorate the wheat harvest and was connected with the giving of the Law in Jesus' day. It was also called the feast of "first fruits." But in the Christian church it became the moment when the power of the Holy Spirit descended upon the early disciples and the church was empowered to go into the world and preach the gospel.

Pentecost is associated with the dramatic events in Acts 2 in which the miracle of hearing and understanding happened—the disciples spoke in tongues and those from all over the world who had come to Jerusalem that day understood what they were saying. Pentecost is a time that emphasizes our world-wide mission to preach the gospel and stresses the importance and presence of the Holy Spirit. That Pentecost 2020 would be a time when division and racial hate erupted was only the latest irony of the strangest year of our collective lives.

Ground Zero

Stop each day to cheer
the heroes leaving work to
work in dreadful fear.

Quarantine

Fear of each other
Loss of all human embrace
Alone together

May-June 2020 Timeline

MAY 2020

May 1: From Michigan to California, gun rights supporters, anti-vaccination activists and business owners protest coronavirus restrictions.

One of the men who brought guns into the Michigan Capitol in late April appears on a live stream from inside. "I don't carry my guns for show. I am not afraid to use them," William Null says. In five months, the FBI charges him and a dozen others in a plot to kidnap Whitmer.

May 15: President Trump announces his administration's vaccine development program. He dubs it Operation Warp Speed.

May 19: Forty-three states have begun at least some form of reopening, hoping to boost their economies. Seven never had stay-at-home orders.

May 24: The virus is surging across rural America, where populations are poorer, older, and more prone to health issues. Rural counties now have some of the highest rates of covid-19 cases and deaths in the country.

May 27: U.S. coronavirus deaths surpass 100,000. The toll goes unmarked by national requiem or collective mourning.

May 31: Millions flood streets across the country to protest the killing of George Floyd and police violence against Black Americans, sparking fears of a new round of virus outbreaks.

JUNE 2020

June 8: In the West and across the South, more than a dozen states set records for new infections reported. Many of these places had avoided the brunt of the pandemic through the spring.

In mid-June, new infections begin a sharp, month-long rise. Unemployment also hits a new level: 13 straight weeks in which more than 1 million people have filed for aid for the first time.

June 25: Americans are living through a split-screen pandemic. The country records its highest-ever single-day case count, yet leaders push ahead with reopening.

June 26: The governors of Texas and Florida reverse course and shut down bars in their states as infections and hospitalizations soar.

The Crucifixion

On a street in Minnesota,
On just another shift,
Showing his new trainees how to keep the peace,
They confront a massive black man, fear in his eyes,
who looks for a way to escape.

Dying under the knee of the leader,
whose leer is frozen for the ages,
he is pinned down by the other three.
"I can't breathe." How plain is that?
The three look at one another, unsure.
They reprise an ancient rendition
Of the street theater of the ages
But this time someone saw. Everyone saw.

He cried out to his mother.
The wrath of God began to swell
into a terrible swift sword
that would strike the streets,
and rip down fraudulent walls
pretending to protect us from our own soul-shadows.

As with every crucifixion,
a man calls out to his mother as he dies,
soldiers laugh and curse,
women weep in despair.
And governors calculate the collateral damage,
wet their index fingers
And lift them to the sky.

A man passing on his way to buy cigarettes
sees the commotion,
shrugs his shoulders and
passes by on the other side of the street.
None of my business, he thinks.

He has no idea.

From My Newsletter Column After the Killing Of George Floyd.

I finally ventured out yesterday to buy some new tennis shoes. Wearing a mask, I went to a local store and followed the rules. I was waited on by a sweet and helpful young woman, also in a mask. She happened to be African American. As I was trying on shoes, I asked, out of habit, "How are you doing?" "Oh, I'm fine, how are you?" A typical exchange of pleasantries.

Something moved me inside to say, "Actually, my heart is broken. That horrible killing of George Floyd in Minneapolis has left me heartsick." And like that, our conversation changed. She opened up, not angry, but surprised that a masked stranger buying tennis shoes would venture the subject, I suppose, but she spoke more frankly that she shared my sadness and a trace of exhaustion. We have to hope and pray things can get better, she said.

It didn't last long, but it reminded me that we can live on the surfaces and not know anything about what's underneath with each other. Something has blown open this week in the soul of our country. It is not new. It is painful, a wound that gets better for a time but never fully heals.

Racism is not only cruel; it is irrational and ultimately brings death and destruction. It is far past time to call it out wherever it is and require our corporate life to reflect who we hope to be at our best—fair for everyone in our society, just in treatment of one another, and fierce to speak out for our neighbor, not just ourselves.

In 1996 Alabama experienced a string of church burnings. Our church made a gift to one of the churches and I drove down to meet with one of the church leaders. Our missions committee donated to them to help rebuild. I wrote these words then, twenty-four years ago. I wish they were not still relevant now. I wish I could say, "That was then, this is now."

> "Racism" is a loaded word. When it is spoken, defenses are erected almost immediately. "Oh, no, some of my best friends are..." Some definitions are so sweeping that they cause despair. Often, African Americans and Anglo-Americans don't even mean the same thing by the word.
>
> Put simply, racism is the irrationally held belief in the inherent superiority of one's own race to all others. Often it is defined to mean an attitude that only those in power can hold against those without power.

I have never doubted in the powerful and pervasive presence of racism, if nothing else from simply moving around a lot. If animosity and political scapegoating had only happened in one place, I would not be so suspicious. But racism, unfortunately, is a fact of life, and not only in America. In virtually every society, the deep-seated need to blame others for our own failings and problems is everywhere.

Many thoughtful and caring people despair that we can ever overcome our hatreds. Through the years, I have never believed that the difficulties of relationships between people could be solved by analysis, though that is a start. It takes more than naming the problem to solve a problem. It takes deeds.

We have not taught the teachings of Jesus vigorously enough. We have not insisted that hatred is incompatible with Christianity… These are not simply "African-Americans." They are fellow Christians. Let us at least say, "Stop it! These are our brothers and sisters in Jesus Christ.

No law will stop hatred, no program overcome it. It must begin inside the human heart, with the determination that we will live the gospel, speak out clearly, teach it consistently and embody Christian love to all. Anything less is little better than the silence that has become our all-too-comfortable pattern. What is required is that we simply follow Jesus whom we profess. Nothing more and nothing less.

Pentecost is the time that symbolizes the breaking of the barriers. On that day, the birthday of the Christian church, people were gathered in Jerusalem for the feast of the harvest in the Jewish faith. What happened was a miracle of understanding, as the gospel was preached across ethnic, language and national barriers.

Irony contains great truth—that America could be demonstrating its oldest pain so openly on the day celebrating Christian barrier-breaking contains a word from the Lord for us. Deeds, not words. Reconciliation takes deeds of healing, acts of mercy and justice, fixing broken buildings and broken laws, dressing wounds, and changing our minds. It is past time.

Let Pentecost be a call to the churches of America to repent of all racism and return to the gospel of Jesus alone as its center. Let us live the words of the Apostle Peter in Acts 10:34-35: "I truly understand that God shows no partiality, but in every nation anyone who fears Him and does what is right is acceptable to Him." The ministry of reconciliation begins in a change of mind and heart. Let us lead the way. My heart is broken, but that is not enough. More is required. This is Pentecost when the wind of God comes from heaven, and we might begin anew.

A Prayer for the World God Loves

Still in the throes of the protests and division over the murder of George Floyd, as outrage, protests, violence and anger broke out everywhere, I prayed this prayer in the church on Sunday, June 7, 2020.

Lord, You sent us out into the world to bring it back to You
that You might show it Your love and make it new.
You chose that we might go into that world
and yet not be of the world in our going.
That is the toughest part,
because a lot of what's wrong with the world
is also what is wrong within all of us, too.

Even as Jesus looked down from the cross
and was able to forge family where there was none,
bringing his mother and John together,
Even as the Holy Spirit brought Peter and Cornelius together
across culture and suspicion and religious prejudice
and made them one in Christ,
so too we yearn to see the miracle of the church again,
a miracle of Christian community,
the miracle of divine Fellowship,
where forgiveness flourishes and life abounds in belonging.
It is the vision to which we aspire
and we ask that You help us to cherish and nourish it
with our very souls and selves.

We pray for humility to remember
that You have fashioned us into Your people
and that apart from You we cannot bear with one another at all.
Give us Your vision to find those who are already seeking You,
and always be ready to welcome them and love them
and help them and pray for them.
And for all the people of the world
give us a breadth of vision
and hearts that have windows and not shutters
and hands that are open
and not closed in fear and distrust and suspicion
and minds not bogged down in justifications and excuses.

We have seen over the past days in our own country O God,

great division and brokenness displayed-- but it was already there.
The wounds were reopened in a terrible event
        and pitted us against one another
at a time when we already have so much to bear.
We pray O God for the spirit of reconciliation,
for calm voices, for listening ears,
for people eager to make peace,
for those who will work for justice
and make sure that it works for everyone.
We pray Loving God for people of all colors
all ethnicities,
to know nothing from Your church but our love
and our willingness to be the bringers of peace.
We pray, dear God, for leaders across our nation,
for governors and mayors and our national leaders,
for community workers
and businesspeople who are struggling to make a go of it.

But out of this moment,
may there come a great moment of opportunity
        that we did not see
that has called us into a different place,
        and to the possibility that You have offered to us.
Rekindle the vision of that which You shared in the scriptures:
"God was in Christ, reconciling the world to Himself,"
and the ministry of reconciliation You gave us.
We have not always discharged this faithfully.
We ask that we might now be those to whom the world points
        and says, "They are the ones who can help."

Be with those who are brokenhearted,
        those who are sad
        those who are angry
        those who are brokenhearted,
That in each case, the deeper need hidden beneath be touched and healed.
The bringers of that vision and hope to the world.
In the name of Jesus we pray, Amen.

Meanwhile, death and grief were overlaid by the pandemic, heightening the difficulties and sorrow that happens regularly in pastoral ministry.

What follows is a song that came to me one day as I was thinking back to the dear, dear people in my ministry who had suffered the loss of a child, and they were many—all unbearable pain that from my viewpoint never really ends in this life. One year there were four different church members who suffered such a loss, the children of different generations—twenties, thirties, and even in their sixties, when a mother still living had to witness it. The hook for this song had been on my mind for a few years since reading a statement from a survivor after a natural disaster who said, "It'll be a long way from here to okay." So, it bubbled up.

Not long after this, a young man in my church, Tyson Stewart, not long out of high school and getting going in life, died tragically, and this song seemed to me to be for him and all the other mothers, fathers, grandparents, siblings and friends and family who walk through "the valley of the shadow of death." I recorded it with my music friends and put it on the music album Mark and I were finishing.

From Here to Okay
June 2020

I was telling my favorite story when I heard a knocking sound
It was my neighbor. He said, "You'd best sit down"
I never finished that story. I'll never tell it again.
The clock on the wall said 7:10.

I'm lost and so angry. She's just sad all the time,
The shadows go with us everywhere.
Now and then for a while we still act like we used to,
But we still can't move that empty chair.

CHORUS:
It'll be a long time before we put it behind us.
Please, just sit with me. There's nothing to say.
Walk with me a while in the valley of grey.
It's a long way from here to okay.

So, thank you so kindly for asking about us
And for the fine food that you brought.

But please take with you the reassuring words you offered,
It's not easy answers I've sought

Some cope with a bottle, and others with a pill,
Some sit in a circle and pray for God's will,
But nothing on earth fills the hole left inside
By a love that was once so alive.

CHORUS:
It'll be a long time before we put it behind us
Please, just sit with me. There's nothing to say.
Walk with me a while in the valley of grey
It's a long way from here to okay (2x)

Communion Prayer
June 24, 2020

O Lord, a table is the most elemental piece of furniture we know.
We sit across and beside and with one another,
share a meal, a story, hopes
and sometimes it is a place of absence with an empty chair
that cannot be filled.
But it is a place of meeting,
the intersection of a family to whom, sooner or later
we come in from the world,
take off our hats and coats, and maybe shoes
and draw close to those we love.

We are here at this table to remember that,
to remember Jesus with the twelve,
who had walked with him three years on the earth.
They had seen and heard and pondered and prayed together
but now they were with him.
and so do we long to be with You, O God,
and with each other.
So, if at this moment we are not in a room together,
use our imaginations—
put faces and names and friends in our hearts and minds
so that in our taking this bread and cup we would feel less alone
less disconnected, less solitary,
and instead encouraged and uplifted.

Let this bread be for us Your body,
an indissoluble bond making us one in spirit and truth,
and may this cup be a sharing in His sufferings,
and in a suffering world and one another's sufferings.
We remember those in need today—
sick, infected, dying, poor, hungry, in trouble.
Wherever they are, however it happened, be with them we pray.
Now bless this bread and this cup. And in the sharing of this meal,
May our hearts burn with a glimmer of recognition
that You are with us. Amen.

A Prayer for the Nation
July 4, 2020

Eternal God,

We are thankful as we recall the events of the founding of this nation
    And the important role Christians played
        in that great experiment of liberty.
We ask that we might have their boldness to stand for principle,
    Their determination to persist in what is right,
    Their charity in tolerance for those with whom they differed,
And their wisdom in creating a society in which difference and conviction
    might abide together.

Help us, we pray, neither to worship the state nor to be cynics toward it,
    Remembering that You gave us authority to enable us to live together
        But that power is given for stewardship,
        not self-enhancement.
    We pray for those in leadership in our nation, states and communities,
        That they would honor the truth
        And live up to the ideals of a democratic society.
    We pray for all who carry the burden and stresses of responsibility
        That their character might endure the tests of time.
        Show them the values of Your Kingdom in their own spiritual walk.
We pray especially on this day for our Vice-President, for health and healing.
    As he faces heart problems.

Help us to be good citizens.
    Help us to honor those in authority
    With our praise and appreciation, surely,
        But even with our questions and dissent.
    Help us to be mindful of the enormous price of freedom,
        Both in lives it has cost and in vigilance on our part.
Save us from conceding to indifference, apathy, sloth or hopelessness.
    Fill us with the passion of conviction
        And the restraint of justice in our dealings
    So that neighbor love might abound toward all.

Deliver us from contempt of neighbor,
And condescension toward those weaker than ourselves,
And grant us merciful hearts when forgiveness is necessary.

We remember this day those in need among us—
    the poor, the broken in spirit,
        The lonely, the sick, and the grief-stricken souls.

We pray especially for our own church family, Lord. We have been hard hit
    with loss in recent weeks,

And this week, one of our children, Tyson Stewart, and one of our elders,
    Betty Longshore.

We pray that they now rest in Your merciful grace.

We mourn the spaces their absences leave
    And for all of the other hard losses in recent weeks.

We know that people everywhere are going through this in the pandemic.
    And with the strangeness of this moment, the losses feel deeper and
    more acute.

Be merciful to us sinners, Lord
    And heal us and heal our land.

May we know Your tender mercies always.

In Jesus' name we pray, Amen.

Shields of Fear
July 11, 2020

All of your life, people afraid,
Bumping into one terror after another,
Nothing stable, and they looked at you
And only saw what was missing.
It caused them to overlook all that was there,
Gifts abounding, keen mind, loving heart,
And a good soul.
Walls and fences and shields,
Carefully designed by adrenaline,
wary of the next enemy,
they forget that in keeping what we fear out
we trap the imaginary enemy on the other side permanently,
Wielding no weapon,
only wanting to be welcomed and loved,
Locked out, trapped in.
And so,

Love waits, patiently, for someone to unbolt the door
and see.

Ordinary Time

Shortly before the explosion of the Space Shuttle Columbia on February 1, 2003, the video and audio feed from inside was filled with boring routine. The astronauts were minutes from their deaths, but they were doing checklists, mugging for the camera, busy working to get ready for landing, and sending pictures out the windows of the super-heated flames of re-entry that would eventually take their lives .

It was that ordinary quality that was striking. One astronaut commented, "No problem. We've got plenty of time." In retrospect that remark is haunting. These were their final moments. The discovery of that tape, a miraculous survivor that fell to earth intact, is a gift, albeit a painful one. And also a reminder that our time is always limited and precious. Every person moving through the routines of a regular day is also living out a precious gift.

While it is unbearable to live every moment in the awareness of death, we might also ask whether it is also unbearable to live life without it. In the awareness of our mortality, every moment of even the dullest routine assumes a sanctity, a preciousness, that charges it with meaning. It also invites us to live our lives for the things that matter. While "ordinary time" in the church year seems to be a 'catch-all" category, it is the place of the most challenging of Christian living—routine.

Politifusing

Daily briefings last
on and on. The numbers rise
as the people talk.

Connectivity

Glued to devices
Exhaustion without labor
Unable to sleep.

A Prayer for Trust
August 1, 2020

You have invited us into the adventure of faith.
    Why is it, then, that we prefer comfort and predictability?

You ask us to trust You
    But we are driving under the influence of the environments of sin.
    It is hard to think
    Of anything but our own selves and what we want.
    If we thought about it the right way,
    If we knew You perfectly, we would not hesitate
    To live full-out in the confidence of faith.

But we are burdened, clouded, unsteady.
    We doubt, like Peter looking down into the dark waters
    Instead of the face of Jesus. And we sink down to the deep.
    We are afraid, and in our fear try to arrange our world
    As to remove our fears completely out of view.

We fashion safety and security as little gods,
    excluding You in the process, along with all that You would give us
    We worry about having enough
    Which leads us to clutch onto what we have
    As though it were ever ours to begin with. And worse,
    We withhold what could bless our brothers and sisters—
    Not only money, which is the easiest thing to give,
    But our time, our priorities, our presence, and our love.

If we would trust You, Loving God, all this must change.
    Help us in that journey.

Today, people's lives are changed by storms and flood, wind and rain.
    Homes are gone, communities are powerless once again.
    It is a discouraging time.

War is going on as usual. And the costs of this time heap up and threaten
    To do us in.

But we should give thanks. When more than now, can we see our
need of You?

What more than this can cause us to reshuffle our lists of what matters?

Turn our hearts, O God, from the things that do not satisfy
    To those which satiate all our thirsts and hungers
    Not only of body but of mind and heart and spirit.

Be with those who need You today—

In the name of Jesus. Amen.

Stuck in the Mud

Stuck in the mud while the Western sun beats down on the fields.
We ran for help down a dirt road with four dogs at our heels.

But It's so good (good, good) to be alive.
Feels so fine (fine, fine) to have arrived.
I'm so glad to see Your face in a smile.

Lost in the desert nobody sure just where to go.
The sun is sinking, and our fuel supply is running low.

But It's so good (good, good) to be alive.
Feels so fine (fine, fine) to have arrived.
I'm so glad to see Your face in a smile.

Tangled in sagebrush, trying hard to get it done.
Fell down a big hole so far I couldn't see the sun.

But It's so good (good, good) to be alive.
Feels so fine (fine, fine) to have arrived.
I'm so glad to see Your face in a smile.

Stuck in the house, quarantined without an end in sight.
There's no escaping each other, we'd better get this right.

and it's so good (good, good) to be alive.
Feels so fine (fine, fine) to have arrived.
I'm so glad to see Your face in a smile.

This little song actually was written while I was in college, about 1976, while I was performing with my first real band. Like the mythical band in the Johnny Cash song, our differences doomed us, and we broke up. But this song was a crowd favorite when we performed. It was imagery from some hilarious and occasionally terrifying experiences while I was a surveyor's rodman in Denver during the summer of 1973. However, there always seemed to be one more verse it needed. Finally, the pandemic gave it to me.

Pastoral Prayer
August 12, 2020

Show us what we cannot yet see.
>We are bound to this earth
>And fettered by time.

We cannot peer past the mists of eternity
>And see where the engines of Your holy kingdom
>Are roaring toward completion.

Speak the words we cannot spell or hear.
>We cover our ears to shut out
>The roar of pain and cries for help
>That threaten to overwhelm us.

Send us the peace we cannot find,
>For our bodies are dulled by sadness and grief,
>Wearied by toil and labor
>And enervated by anxious fears.

We have come here today not merely to pray and preach
>About hope, but to find some.

This day we come and hear in these scriptures Your reminder to us
That Your ways are higher than ours.
We look at the outward appearance and make our judgments.
You look into our hearts and character and
being and draw us into deeper living.
We look at what is and adjust to it.
>You heal us and show us new things that we never imagined.

We forget too quickly that to live is to grow and learn and change.
>And if we settle too easily for security at the price of life, forgive us.

Help us, like Jesus, to see the possibilities in those around us.
For our Youth and children, we pray that we might
>Recognize their gifts, acknowledge their aspirations, bless their efforts, and hear their questions.
>Help us neither to stand in their way nor abandon them.
>Teach us how to affirm them without abdicating our responsibility to discipline and protect them.

Help us to be quick to bless, slow to criticize and ready to understand.
>May our correction be always done in a spirit that invites them toward responsibility and maturity.

For all the children and youth of the world we pray.

That they might know the full and abundant life that You wish to give us all.
Help us to work with all our might for that life to be true for all.
We are most thankful for Christian community and for this fellowship
> May our children remember always that here they were loved.
> May they never forget that here they were told the story of Jesus.
> May they always know this as a community that takes up crosses
>> And not merely explains them to us.
>> In Jesus' name. Amen.

Pastoral Prayer
August 19, 2020

Lord God,
You have taught us that our lives are not meant for standing but walking.
    We are always moving as Your people, down the road
    Between the waters of the sea, across the wilderness,
    through the night
Toward the promised land and heaven.
Thank You first for walking with us along the way, teaching us,
    encouraging us
    And stopping us from certain death when we walk the wrong way.
For Christ, who came and walked with us to Jerusalem and then
    walked on alone
    Where none of us could go.
    He went on to the cross and into the grave
    And back again—a journey none of us could withstand.
He came back to give us good news.
Now our going is no longer our own. We go where You want us to go.
    We go where needs are. We go where Your leadership takes us….

Help us to live faithfully, so that we would not bring shame upon Your name.
This is the hard part about this time. We have to space out, walk down one
    aisle and up the next,
Respect others' space and live our walk in a time when caution is the word.
We are called to walk in patience when irritation is as great as sickness
We are called to walk in hope when emptiness, death and tragedy
    are everywhere
We are called to walk in faith though the path is not clear, and leaders divided.
We are called to walk in love though anger rolls across our land
    like thunderclouds
    Made of frustration and misinformation and confusion.
We are called to walk in prayer though our anxiety wants to sit by the
    television hoping for a miracle
    rather than the tedium of waiting for answers.
We come this day to remember that we never walk alone
    We walk here because of those who went before us
    Went through times worse than these.

We walk because staying where we are is not a choice.

We pray for those who are lame, broken and limping with sorrow, sadness, depression and loneliness.
We pray for our young children and students to walk safely
and for their protection
We pray for our families and all families, coping with so much to know
We pray to walk with open hands, ready to give, share, assist and care.
We ask for merciful reminders that You are able to supply our every need.
In Jesus' name, Amen.

Dust Storm
August 23, 2020

A cloud rolls toward the house from the east.
It swallows the desert sand, billowing and terrible,
Angry wall, blotting out light, sand and fury.
We hurriedly tape the doorjambs and window edges,
Close the chimney flue
And wait.
A moan echoes in the chimney.
It covers the midday sun.
Dark shadow-line races toward us
and swallows the house ahead of the sand. It is night.
How long can we breathe? How much water did we store?
Do we have enough food?

The last time we had one of these
We came out and cleaned up,
Swept every iota of dirt and fine dust out
And swore we'd do better next time,
But we forgot as good days followed one another
And the urgency faded.
Now it seems as though it has brought
Seven more just like it.
And there is nothing to do but wait and hope
And pray for one more deliverance.

Repent
August 24, 2020

"Okay. I promise."

"This time…" for the thousandth time.
Don't look back.
"Today can be the first day of the rest…"
Failure is cumulative in the soul,
        Whether you're a serial shopper, wife beater
        Overeater, sex addict, thief or raging fool.
It hangs around like a terrible odor.

I'd rather forgive seven times seventy
A thousand times
than face a slough full of disgust and self-loathing.
                For one, you can perch on a lofty place,
                      look down, unaffected by the pain of
                      another.

If you can avoid the need to repent of that…

Opening
August 25, 2020

Reconciliation only happens
when there is a way through the wall
that keeps you out and me in.
"Something there is that doesn't love a wall,"
especially ones that kill us both in the end.

Pastoral Prayer
August 25, 2020

Mighty God, we affirm that You are the Creator,
       That worlds came into being at Your command;
That ocean tides and countless suns move in consonance with
       Your vast and intricate rhythms of purpose.
We believe that from nothing came creation
       And that it is sustained and upheld by Your might.

Why, then, do we struggle so as we face our own difficulties?
       Why do our spiritual knees wobble when trouble comes?
Do we not know that as You refashioned Israel
to bring her from exile,
       You can also make us new?
Why do we hold onto our sins after You have put them
       as far as east from west?
       Do we not remember that when we are in You
       There is a new creation, a new day, and new possibilities?

Why do we continue to live by the scripts others write for us,
the stereotypes that press on us, the past they will not remove from us?
Why do we struggle so to believe and know that Your Spirit still moves today
as it moved on the watery depths of Creation itself?

Help us, O God, to believe that there are ways yet unknown to us,
       Paths we have not yet walked,
       Possibilities we have not envisioned
And new creation that only awaits Your marvelous and miraculous
       Time to come forth.

May we serve You not in absolute certainty so much as
       Undying devotion. When we are stopped in our tracks,
       Help us to look for You.
When we are broken, may we expect You to appear.
When we are down, may we lift up our heads and look for redemption.
Through Jesus Christ our Lord, Amen.

Pastoral Prayer
September 9, 2020

Lord, Creator and Savior,
We have known Your abundance throughout life.
When we sit and take time to list our gratitude, it grows longer as we consider it.
We count ourselves, most of us here and in this community,
as most fortunate by birth
And our hard work has usually been rewarded.
We are glad about so much, even now with all of this.
So, when we ask for help, we recognize that we have little room to complain.
Give us the Holy Spirit so that we would not ask for the wrong things.
Help us in the things that matter.
We know we're in a fix that only You can help,
and the deepest concerns of our hearts are not just ourselves—
it is people we love, some sick, some dying,
Some are soaked with grief and sorrow,
some so down they can't muster a prayer.
We need help because we don't know where to start.
We're worried about our children
and the world we live in, and the way it's going and the way we're all acting
We should be pulling the rope together instead of lashing each other
Listening instead of scorning others we don't know.
And we know You are at work, we count on that.

But tell us what our part is, how we enter into this mystery
Of hurting with those who hurt and leading them to wholeness
How to care
without being consumed and overwhelmed and too tired to do it anymore.
Help us to weep if we need to, and then get up and get going again.
We have a long way to go.
Help our congregation and its people.
Help us in our struggles.
Help our country.
Help this world of trouble and trials.
Help the scientists who are working nonstop
And help nurses who come home and fall in bed.
Help doctors who can't take one more shift.

Help leaders who want to quit and children who are sad.
Help mothers who are discouraged and fathers who are preoccupied.
We still have bedtime stories to read and reassurance to offer.
Help us keep this church going, because we all need it more than we realize.
Help our families to stay together.
Help our marriages to weather the storms.
Help the poor to hang on one more day.
Help us all, Lord,
not to be distracted into ourselves.

Help us, each, to hear Your call in our lives.
You ask us all to do something for You in this life.
      Help us to hear it. But more importantly, when we hear it
not to dismiss it or shrink it down to our size or resist it.
Just to answer and go when we know it's You.
      Help Your people in the world today who did answer.
They are all over this world this morning, and many of them are struggling
We pray for the gospel to be blessed and multiplied

Help us, O God, to care in these careless times.
      Amen.

Like all who were able, we did a lot of video binging during 2020. After watching a bio documentary of the architect's life, this poem.

Frank Lloyd Wright
September 15, 2020

Fascinating, interesting, vexing, brilliant, troubled,
Vain, condescending, indifferent, pain causing
Arrogant, cruel and insufferable, gifted of God
from whom breathless splendor was left for the world.
He imposed his vision to every onlooker,
helped them to look to earth and sky
and feel heaven in water and rocks and floors and wood
and grass so real it hurt the feet to tread.

Blood of tragedy in the nearby ground,
woman from whom he came
and woman whose love was taken from him,
lie side by side in asymmetry,
with his small remains next to them in eternal mystery.
He rests in the earth on which all shelter stands
amid the dust to which every architect, save One, returns.

Something like him lives in every soul,
Ugly, eternal, light-bearing, boasting ego,
yearning to make its gifts seen
radiating glory when they break free,
wrestling with pain and joy
in hopes that they will hold hands at last.

Pastoral Prayer
September 16, 2020

O God,
        You spoke in the quietness of the desert to Moses
        In the quiet cave You spoke to Elijah
        In the quiet places of our hearts, speak and we will listen.

        Our minds are not empty--they are too full.
They are full of uncertainty and stress and strain.
        They are overloaded with worry about people we love
            And trouble all over the world
            and fear of what else will come.
Our ears are full of noise—of arguments and contention,
        of blame and resentment.
Our eyes are full of images of raging fires and weeping mothers
        Of homeless families and angry divisions.
Our hearts are full of grief and sorrow and fear of the unknown.
Empty us, O God, so that in the stillness You might speak
        and we might hear a word from You.

Our days are not empty--they are crowded with devices
and zoom meetings and links and calls.
They are filled with daily tasks that are no longer simple.
Everything is harder and takes longer.
        And they are filled with frustration at the obstacles
        And impatience for cures and solutions
        And irritation on the highway and at home.
        And boredom with the imprisonment of our caution.

Empty us, O God, of our disquiet and restlessness
        that rob us of joy and blind us to the beauty of creation around us
        and within.

        Our consciences are not empty--
            they are full of accusing memories;
Sins we cannot blot out without Your help.
        We are paralyzed by the consequences of our choices
        And the damage from our way of life.

Empty us, O God, by the forgiving power of the cross;
    blot out our sins and cleanse us, set us free.
    set us before us, clothed in Christ and in our right minds
This day we come with great thanksgiving
    for those who model Your simplicity,
    for saints who show us how to pray,
and spiritual friends who uphold us when we stumble,
and the comfort of Your people who love us always.
Today we pray for all the people
whose hearts and minds and eyes and ears are crowded like ours.
May they be set at liberty
through Christ our Lord. Amen

Pastoral Prayer
October 7, 2020

Gracious Lord,
In our praying we remember the truth:
that we are made to be connected to You and connected to one another.
In this text we are amazed that Paul, in prison and perhaps about to die
was not alone and knew it. His heart was still full of giving to others
      And full of joy about You. He was not alone.
We pray that we would know what it means to live in such connection,
to know that
What we do and say and live out releases power to those around us
or withholds it from them.
What happens to others in our lives and on the other side of the world
is inevitably part of us.
We are not alone. We have been saved into fellowship,
Been given the company of Your spirit and
a community of believers to whom we belong.
Yet sometimes—whether under the pressures of depression or anxiety
or the forgetfulness of sin--
      we live as though we were all alone.
We make decisions as though no one else were with us.
We blot out the memories of Your goodness
We choose as though we were the only person in the world.
We pursue courses of action for our own interests without any consideration
of the vast and devastating impact our selfishness can have.
Even in simply withdrawing from one another,
pulling back in our wounds and vowing
      That we will have to do with others no more, quitting a relationship,
becoming angry and withdrawn.
We renounce our confidence that all things will one day be healed and reconciled.
Sometimes our sin is giving up hope, losing confidence, and resigning from life.
Whether out of fear or selfishness,
we realize that sin was born out of these motives.
Save us from disconnection. Forgive us for the damage we have already done
      The work we have failed to do, the hope we have abandoned.

Remind us of the power of the Holy Spirit You sent into our lives.

    Forgive us for going it alone, for giving up on each other, for giving into despair or grief

    Or pain so that we quit on the path of redemption.

Help us not to quit or be quitters. Remind us of the richness of relationship that is our joy to possess.

Connect us this day with the needs of others—

For world leaders who struggle for peace, especially our President and the leaders of nations battling with disease and hardships and fear. Grant them eyes to see and ears to hear the cries of hurting people.

    May they discover at least in just dealings to live with one another

We pray for Christians in the world who live in prison cells of a culture that misunderstands and hates them.

Bless all those who labor as Your church in the world.

These things we pray in the name of Jesus, Amen.

Pastoral Prayer in Stewardship Season
October 14, 2020

God, Our Provider,
We have been the recipients of Your goodness
You have blessed us, literally, materially, abundantly.
Help us to be good stewards of Your blessings,
remembering that we are accountable for our stewardship.
Even now, in this time of disruption, we have found blessing,
Help us to be stewards of the mystery You have entrusted to us--the gospel.
Strengthen our commitment and resolve to serve You in every
sphere of our lives. Now of all times we need it most.
As we make our commitments together to our church life, O Lord,
I pray only that the same spirit of unity, faith and generosity
that we have known in recent years might prevail once more.
Our church budget is only part of what You do through us,
but it is a visible and important expression of our commitment
to teach the faith to the next generation, to worship You in holiness,
to serve through caring ministries and to give Your love to the world.

Guide our families as they manage their lives and homes, health and choices.
Guide us each to do what we are able and willing to do for the Kingdom,
not simply to further Your work here through this church.
Thank You for our abundant resources
not only money, but time, talents, intelligence and spiritual gifts.
May we use them all as reflectors of Your glory.

Help us to be stewards in society.
Guide us as we struggle with decisions as a nation and as a state
to elect new leadership and decide on matters that affect us.
Grant us clarity of heart and mind
as we make our choices in an imperfect world
and grant us the civility to listen when others disagree
and to consider in humility whether we are wrong,
grace to accept our collective decisions and to work with all
for the good of all.

Now bless us here as we worship You,
that we might reap spiritual abundance
and blessings of heart and soul and mind. In Jesus name.

Pastoral Prayer
Children's' Sabbath Sunday, October 21, 2020

Loving Creator, whose loving passion made the world,
On this day we remember families and children.
The faces that are near us are our own children,
And it is looking on them that we understand sacrifice and love most deeply.
Love for them is biologically planted in us.
  But on this day we pray that You would expand our love outward,
  We need Your help for that.
In this time we can only look with screens and our hearts and prayers,
But we know they are everywhere in this world.
Give us hearts open and overflowing to care for all the children of this world
That we would see them as You see them and
  Love them with our time and resources and vision
And devote ourselves as Your church to their spiritual well-being
Whether that means teaching them the gospel or building a school
  Feeding them or giving them the bread of life.
We pray to understand what Your will in this troubled world is for us
  And that we would have the faith of Jesus to do it,
  The love of Jesus to do it gladly,
  And the courage of Jesus to do it no matter what the cost.
As Your church in this place, help us to give our energies and resources
  More and more to making a difference in our world,
  To advocating for what is best and right and true and fair,
  And caring about those who are forgotten and neglected and in pain.
Show us the pathways of caring that are our calling here.
Lord, we pray for health and peace and prosperity
  But even more for equity, and decency and generosity,
That ours could become the world You see as possible,
  That suffering be ameliorated, kindness multiplied
  And families strengthened and upheld by what we choose and do.
Please minister through us to our own children to teach them the gospel
  Model the kingdom and lift up love of neighbor as our way.
We pray for all in Your world who are wounded and battered by troubles
  Wars, pain and sorrow.

May there be genuine peace and lasting justice
>	And may each of us, in our praying and going and ministry
>	And voting and advocating and caring
>	Be the instruments by which it is done. In Jesus' name. Amen.

Quiet: A Reflection

There are three moments that come to my mind when I ponder the word silence. The first was when a spiritual director friend began to introduce me to contemplative silence by the discipline of being quiet intentionally for 5 minutes. Whenever we met, we would begin with his lighting of a candle, the scent of which continues to take me to prayerfulness now. Then he would set a timer after reading a scripture and we would be quiet for 5 minutes together.

It was excruciating. My mind is like an entire cage full of monkeys on steroids. But eventually I begin to grow still and that led me to a 5-day silent retreat. A new world opened up.

The second time, oddly enough, was at Epcot center in Orlando Florida. Many years ago, I would go annually to Florida for a clergy conference at Stetson University. It was in the winter when sunny Florida was the perfect place to be.

I was at Epcot on a ride, I can't remember which because it was so long ago, but maybe it was the one where you go through paleo history and see automated dinosaurs and all sorts of other things that overwhelm you with the deceptions of human virtual ingenuity. After riding through the fake world, I was going up an incline and was able to see behind a curtain of some kind. I saw ordinary things, something a workman had left behind a door and a plain 60 watt lightbulb. The spell was broken. I saw the machinery behind the illusion and a deep despair settled over me.

The third scene was at the end of my doctoral work at Baylor University. I had labored for 6 years to achieve a goal I had held since high school to get an advanced academic degree in Christian thought. Graduation day was a heady and extraordinary experience. I felt a profound sense of blessing my major professor blessed me. My wife and children, who sacrificed so much for me, and my parents were there. It was a moment of euphoria and actually that euphoria would last for a number of weeks on and off but then for just a bit the strangest thing happened.

I was walking across the campus after it was all over, and the others had gone on home. Now the campus was still. And there was this great sense that everything was empty, no energy in the rooms. The buildings were dark, and people were driving away. And again, that gnawing emptiness.

I have always felt the same realization at these moments. It comes as a question. Is there genuine presence at the center of things or is it a dead and mechanical universe? No originality in that thought but it agonizes me to ponder it. There are times when I have been in death's presence when the universe seemed alive and full of mystery. At other times, there was only a cold, clinical stillness, a living being now absent of what we call life, and now only motionlessness.

Quiet can be rich, it can be terrifying. It is, for me, the genuine original mystery for which my faith seeks answers. Is Someone there or not? Is something still living when what is here is gone? And in a pandemic silence now falls upon the earth anew, some as terrible loneliness, some as extinguished breath, and still some as forced solitude.

Musicians often talk about leaving enough space between the notes so that the hearer's ear is not so full of noise that the note can do its work. Silences (in musical notation, oddly enough, called "rests,") are indispensable if we are not to produce endless noise.

The pandemic brought many things, but one unexpected one was the silences. Funerals without visitations, hundreds of thousands of deaths without explanations or deathbed reconciliations, a quarantined world, its traffic stilled and an eerie forced sabbath from human self-created activity. The economies of the world ground to temporary halt, people working from home were without the watercooler and the lunchtime with others.

Let's face it, humanity was unnerved. The silence was overwhelming.

Empty Spaces
October 26, 2020

Empty spaces fascinate me.
Of course, without "filled spaces", what do they really mean?
Even if immense parts of the universe are only "void,"
it is the moving pieces, vectors, protons, waves,
particles, places, people, the complexities that intrigue me
or even make the empty space comprehensible.

Empty spaces are understandable—but
why anything *at all* dotting the spaces here and there?
Why are entities "there?"

And what is it that moves me to fill these spaces while I wait?
Why strike up a conversation I would not have set out to have,
observe the waiting
or record the moment of emptiness?

It is as though both note and silence
drive me mad with their necessity.

November 2020 Timeline

Nov. 3: It is Election Day, and many Americans already have cast their ballots in a record-setting, pandemic-spurred wave of early voting.

Nov. 7: Joe Biden wins the presidential election, officially inheriting the public health crisis as the country enters the worst-yet stretch of the pandemic. President Trump refuses to concede and will insist for months that the election was "rigged." His scores of lawsuits will be rejected, including at the Supreme Court.

Nov. 9: Pfizer-BioNTech reports that its vaccine is more than 90 percent effective at protecting people from the virus. A week later, Moderna reports that its vaccine is nearly 95 percent effective, a sign that the country could have two vaccines by the end of the year.

Nov. 19: The day the death toll reaches 250,000, the CDC urges Americans to avoid travel and gatherings during the Thanksgiving holiday, warning that those activities could supercharge virus spread.

Nov. 23: Americans don't listen. Air travel reaches an all-time pandemic high. Exactly two weeks later, the country is recording an average of 200,000 new infections every day — precisely the surge experts feared.

Georgia leaders reject President Trump's push to overturn election results.

Pastoral Prayer
All Saints Sunday, November 2020

Dear God, what can we bring to this day except gifts of gratitude
    For Your extravagant grace.
In this week in which the churches of the world remember their Saints,
    All those who have gone before us and prepared the way
    By their faith, work and hopes and love.
And now, after their deaths, become part of the great cloud of witnesses
    who surround us in this dangerous spiritual journey on earth.
We are still in the struggle they have finished, so help us.
    We confess that sin still clings to us,
    Its habits, its fears, its distortions and lies
    And in our anxieties and frailty, we stumble and fail You.
Forgive us, Lord, and fill us with faith
    So that we might live for what really is
    Instead of what seems to be.
Forgive us for the hurts we have done to one another
    whether intentional or neglectful and oblivious.
Awaken our love for what is good so that we do not want sin any more.

We remember this day those in need among us—the poor, the broken in spirit,
    The lonely, the sick, and the grief-stricken souls.
    May they know Your tender mercies always.

In Jesus' name we pray, Amen.

This song came out one evening while I was, like millions of grandparents and family members everywhere, grieving the separations caused by a global pandemic. The reunion came after we'd missed birthdays, holidays and important times. But it finally came....

I Hope We'll Be Together
November 1, 2020

1. I hope we'll be together sometime soon.
Tell the same old stories round the room.
We'll hold the babies on our laps,
And after lunch we'll grab a nap,
Tell each other things we hope to do.

2. But a deadly winter storm is coming on.
We'll have to stay here at the house until it's gone.
First Thanksgiving Day we've missed,
But life is hard sometimes like this,
We'll hunker down and call you on the phone

CHORUS:
Don't worry little darlings, we're right here.
Hope is greater than the darkest fear.
Friends and faith and family ties
Hold us up and make us wise.
I hope we'll be together next year.

3. And if somehow, we don't make it through,
I want you to remember I told you,
Nothing else means more to me
Than the treasure chest of memories
of reasons in my heart why I love you.

CHORUS:

tag
Face to face or in Your hearts, nothing will keep us apart
One way or another, next year.

Living Memory
November 18, 2020

History does not belong to victors
Nor the vanquished,
Or even the historiographers
(and certainly not the journalists who serve us the
daily breaking news).

The history we fight over, kill one another for, is
Biased with group grievances;
piled up with the force of government,
mythology and editorial control.

The Story, though, is remembered everywhere
Official and casual, annals and folklore
The upward thrust recorded by Darwin
And the dark side of the Force by Paul and Augustine.

It is kept by families and tribes
In boxes on shelves and in attics, even crevices of the floor
Dirty little secrets are kept in closets, of course,
Stuck under beds and behind doors
Hastily shoved into pockets when we carry them around.

The worst truths are put away.
Painful ones are stuffed in the attic.
It takes effort to find them and pull them out
And the most shameful ones are down in the basement,
Near the furnace, in damp and scary places
Where none but the brave and innocent go.

The rest, the invisible ones, have long seeped
Into our genes and serpentine brains
Escaping now and then into rage and terror
Unknown but familiar when they burst out of our chests,
Quickly forgotten, ever-present
Who could possibly tell it all in a book?
Or teach it to children truthfully?

As America embroiled itself in conflict and division, my mind went back to a famous and horrifying photograph I had seen as a student many years ago from the end of World War II.

The Desecration of Mussolini
November 19, 2020

Stomping the head of the lifeless torso
an unnamed man channels the rage of the mob
with his heel on behalf of a suffering nation.
The head recoils but does not respond.
The sunken eyes stare nowhere.

How could we have let this happen?
Who gave their consent for this man,
this pompous and crafty wizard,
to beguile us until we ended up here
on a street filled with grief, undone
by the state of our collusion with Death and deviance
and the powerlessness that comes
from ceding our choices out of indifference or simple weariness?

The seducers let themselves in by unlocked basement doors
and stand like roosters, preening on the balcony
before crowds of the hoi polloi.
But we talk ourselves into seduction,
Destruction, reduction, corruption, cheering wildly.
Did we know? Did we just not want to know,
That we would end up in a jeering mob,
no longer looking up in adoration, but
now staring down at a pile of abused cadavers
as a furious foot is bent on proving he can hurt us no more?

How could we who call the name of the Crucified
not remember again what emptiness comes
from the negotiations with Pilate?

Advent

Advent is the period of four Sundays prior to Christmas day. Advent is a time of waiting. It corresponds imperfectly to the anxious anticipation of children "awaiting their rewards," because the waiting of our children is a waiting not born of desperation like that first Advent. The first advent (literally "coming into the world") was the coming of Christ.

The coming of baby Jesus was not a celebration of childbirth nor of innocence and joy. His coming was the entry of light into darkness, ignorance, and sin. His life was threatened even in infancy by the powers of his time. He grew up amid people whose daily lives were suffocating under Roman tyranny.

In the history of the church, therefore, Advent was traditionally known as a penitential, not a celebrative, season. It is a time of preparation and repentance, much like the message of John the Baptist who prepared the way for the coming of the Messiah. The dominant color of Advent is purple, a color typically associated with repentance and sorrow. Yet even as we prepare, there is anticipation of joy to come--the hope that burns brightly in us that life can be better for all.

New Normal

Planners meet daily
to anticipate and plan
what cannot be known.

Waiting

Televangelists
sit in empty rooms just like
those with little faith.

Stars and Stripes
Gary Allison Furr, November 30, 2020

An 18-wheeler pulling flammable liquid roars by my car.
Just behind the cab, a pair of big American flags
snapping in the wind
on flexible poles
they strain backwards from the wind resistance
worn and frayed at the edges.

It's in my face at car level,
I don't know what to think.
He whips the rig in front of me, almost cutting my front bumper off,
and roars on.

The flag I have waved, which gave me a lump in my throat
       after the terrorists killed my fellow citizens,
            now leaves me confused.

Does it invite me to be grateful?
Or just go to hell?
Does he mean for me to love it?
Shove it?
Or just think proud thoughts of it?
Do the flags mean, "I served and I'm proud?"
I love my country and I'd die for all of you?
Or just a way to say,
 "Yeah? Well, **** you, too."

And why me? Or this random assortment
of hurried people on Thanksgiving Day?
What spurred you to do this?
Or did your boss insist
You hoist them as his balled-up fist?
And what of my own anger
so quick to surface at any perceived slight
       in the day or in the night?

Did Betsy Ross know that
her proud accomplishment
would be flapping near the sound
of a loud diesel exhaust vent someday
as the driver cuts in front
of confused pilgrims to deliver
his explosive load
and go home,
while those in vehicles too small to take him on
      vent their own anger alone?

Pastoral Prayer
Advent, December 1, 2020

Somewhere today, a house is silent.
A loved one died of this disease, and they weren't prepared to accept it.
At a hospital, exhausted nurses and support staff are scrubbing,
hoping they aren't carrying the virus home.
On the other side of the world, Christians worship amid hostility and suspicion.
In London or Las Vegas or a small town in the Appalachians,
a young woman did drugs and will wake up later today
and start desperately looking for her next fix.
In Washington, leaders struggle to find solutions
and hope that an election just past is a turning point.
Lots of families went to bed hungry. Lots of people went to bed angry.
Someone lost their job. A business owner had to let them go,
and the business is in a hard spot.
He doesn't know exactly how to keep going.
Someone moved out of the house and gave up on a marriage.
Someone else decided to wait one more day.
Grieving people are exhausted from crying.
Hopeless people are praying in desperation.
Frazzled people are trying to keep a business in trouble going.
Every moment, every day, the world of need passes by
If we consider its pleas of our own strength, Lord,
we will collapse from its weight.
We cannot raise enough money, send enough people
or solve enough problems to help this world.

In this moment, we join our hearts and minds and bodies,
not even able to work together to do it.
But we believe, against all detractors,
that putting our prayers with all that hurt does something that only You understand,
We send money and make phone calls to help through others.
It feels like we did something, because we know that there is a connector in the world.
The Spirit abides with us, upholds us, cries with us, pleads for us,
holds onto us. And we put our own heads and hearts into these moments and beg
because we love You. You have shown us the way.
You have promised help to us.

Help those we are trying to help. Be through us what You need.
Multiply our energies to marshal great radiant beams of love and hope.
touch minds seeking answers.
Lift spirits that are dragging the ground.
Let us be here at least with them all, with You in You, all of us together
This day. For the cause of Christ
In the name of Jesus. By the power of the Spirit. Amen.

Pastoral Prayer *Advent 3*
December 12, 2020

Lord, today our hearts are filled by the scriptures,
listening to Mary sing from the joy of new life inside her.
The world around was hard as a stone and filled with cruelty,
life was harsh and without much hope.
But this young woman, faithful in her dilemma
was the one You chose to carry the hope of humankind.
You are always a step ahead of our tiresome categories.
You choose the people we write off.
You see the promise and the beauty hidden from our eyes.
We are separated from Your vision by
hardness of heart, being in a hurry, failure to listen,
stubbornness, self-will, all of that.
We make it so hard for ourselves, and it makes no sense.
You offer everything to us.
You give us all we have. You love us with everlasting love.
Do we really believe we know better than You?
Do we actually think we can reinvent truth and reality?
So today we try again to see a young girl and identify with her—
alone, uncertain, and unimportant.
Teach us how to see her, listen to what she has to say,
take the time to understand her,
learn from her.
There are things greater and more powerful than all the armies of the world:
A kingdom of love and grace and truth
A savior who suffers.
A church that follows.
A forgiveness that changes.
A hope that stands.

In this Advent season, help us to see this young girl,
really see her, and believe as she does
That Your purposes are not thwarted by our indifference to them.
Your will is not prevented by human opposition and sin.
You are beyond all preachers and systems and influencers
podcasters and power brokers.
Teach us to accept Your truth as ours.

Show us how to love as You loved in Jesus Christ.
Show us the way of Your kingdom.
Give us eyes and ears to notice the humble and the poor.
Lord we bring our hearts, our hopes, our fears, our pain, and our sorrow
and leave them here with You.
We hold up to You our disappointments and sins
our troubles and hurts and ask You to help us.
We lift up the pain of the world
that crushes us under our load of concern and beg You
To help where we cannot, to heal through our prayers and giving and help.
To love through our service and acts of kindness.
To sustain through our calls and cards and emails and texts.
    In these days,
we are raw with disagreement in our country, hard feelings and contention,
We are weary of staying in, fearful of going out,
exhausted by waiting for answers that now
we learn are farther away than we thought.
It is a time of testing, but we're tired of being tested.
Help us.
    In the name of Jesus who loved us first. Amen.

Christmas

Web of Fear

Nightmares rise up now,
inflame the stupored hearers
with disinformation.

Nature Breathes

The earth rests from us.
Our noise has ceased from the land.
Creation is glad.

My Last Christmas Eve

This would be my last Christmas as Pastor of the church. The Advent and Christmas seasons were always my favorites at our church—filled with joy and anticipation and tradition. The visual elements were always prominent and beautiful—poinsettias and spectacular floral arrangements, the Advent wreath and Christmas tree with Chrismons. The church did not yet know, but it mattered greatly to me.

The most meaningful part of the season was always the Christmas Eve communion. We would have a lovely informal service for children, dressed as little angels, shepherds and sheep, at 5, then a traditional candlelight service. The handbells played "Infant Holy, Infant Lowly", my personal favorite. At the end of the service, the choir, including any former choir members who'd come home, would circle up at the back of the sanctuary and sing Norman Luboff's lovely "Still, Still, Still" after we'd concluded "Silent Night" with lit candles. The candlelight part was so nerve wracking to Jim St. John, the city fire chief, that he'd never attend.

Numbers were spiking in Jefferson County, and, like other churches, we went back to online only for a few weeks until the surge abated. But on Christmas Eve, though it was virtual, we re-enacted it as close to the way we'd always done it. I was overwhelmed with the coming change in my life and this church. But I was filled with gratitude, too. "My church." That's what I call them, but they're not mine. This is God's church. We made it through the year, somehow. And a lot of credit went to the people of the church. They loved their church and one another. They stayed together, gave faithfully, did all they could. The great gift of 2020 was for pastor and staff to learn an important lesson: there is a church even without programs, activity and normal advantages. I really love this strange motley collection of people who have stuck it out together. It did not happen without its challenges, but an enormous amount of change happened without an implosion.

I suspect this was a discovery in churches everywhere. Maybe it was not as shiny and exciting as preachers tried so hard to make it, but it was better. When you get down to it, the Incarnation is the important fact about church: Christ in you, the hope of glory, clay feet and all.

So, I led communion on TV, the final Christmas Eve of this chapter of my life. For the musicians, staff, and handful of helpers who came, it was glorious. We turned up the lights, blasted the heat and used our imaginations to remember the good days behind and hope for good ones to come.

Pastoral Prayer
January 4, 2021

Lord we come this day as Your people,
at the beginning of a new calendar year.
But while the calendar has changed our situation has not.
Troubles surround our world and our nation.
What has also not changed is Your divine Love,
Your great purposes, Your merciful offer of grace,
the power of forgiveness, the goodness of the gospel,
and the hidden million acts of service that Your people do every day.

We pray for our nation and for families stricken by death and loss
We pray for nurses, worn out at the end of shifts, and for doctors and administrators, exhausted by the pandemic but also by our nation,
fighting against one another,
disregarding the realities of the moment,
anxious and angry sometimes or despairing in others.
We pray for families, trying hard to carry out their responsibilities
but weary with the complexity of it.
We pray for people who love You and even those who don't,
and for those who do harm to Your Kingdom in Your name,
that they might wake up and see the truth while they have time.

We pray for Your church, here, and everywhere, trying to hold up the faith
when there is deepening distrust and misunderstanding and blame all around.
Help us to be the calm peacemakers and the defenders of righteousness.

We pray for the lonely and disconnected.
For those mired in depression,
for those struggling to pay bills and hold marriages together,
for those scrambling to climb out of trouble. Amen.

Epiphany

"Epiphany" is a strange word. This might help: You probably have said or heard someone say, "I had an epiphany." That usually means, "It just came to me. It wasn't reasoned out, just all of a sudden I knew." Epiphany is a word that means "manifestation," when something extraordinary is made known. Moses and the burning bush is an epiphany story. So is Elijah and the still small voice. It's a time when God makes Himself known to us.

Selfies

People do research
On Facebook and internet
To determine facts.

Childhood Regrets

Scientists were nerds
We made fun of during school
Now we have regrets.

As if enough terrible things had not fallen on the world and America, a bizarre and determined band of extremists saw a rally in Washington as a call to violence and destruction. The rage over the election result for President boiled over into an attack on the Capitol itself. The perpetrators saw it in their minds as some kind of justified revolution. They beat policemen and stormed the building, seeking political opponents and threatening even the vice-President, who was hurried away by Secret Service agents. It unfolded in front of the horrified nation. I have included only two sermons in this volume, this one and my final one. This one touched a chord for many who heard it, and I hope it will inspire readers to consider the responsibility of our words. We all fail many times to use them for good, but at least we can remember their power to heal or to wound.

"Choice Words"
Matthew 12:33-37

Sermon preached on Sunday, January 10, 2021, at Vestavia Hills Baptist Church by Dr. Gary Furr, pastor.

> *33 "Either make the tree good, and its fruit good; or make the tree bad, and its fruit bad; for the tree is known by its fruit. 34 You brood of vipers! How can you speak good things, when you are evil? For out of the abundance of the heart the mouth speaks. 35 The good person brings good things out of a good treasure, and the evil person brings evil things out of an evil treasure. 36 I tell you, on the day of judgment you will have to give an account for every careless word you utter; 37 for by your words you will be justified, and by your words you will be condemned."*

Think about the lowly wedge for a moment. Carpenters, of which I was for many years during school, use them all the time. A wedge is a long triangular piece of wood. You can buy them now, but we cut them out of boards ourselves in my short career as a carpenter. They start as a rectangle but get narrower and narrower until they come to a point.

When we installed doors and windows, we used small wedges to hold the doorframe in place until we had it right in place. A tap here or there drove it a little farther in to move the frame this way or that. We all use them every time we put a rubber doorstop under a door to hold it open. It is a lowly task, having people kick you over and over just so you can hold the door for them.

If doorstops could speak, they would complain that it's all about the rest of us. They are servants. And in a church, they hold the doors while elderly members go out of the sanctuary on their walkers and canes or while funeral directors wheel the body of someone we love out to the hearse for the procession to the cemetery.

So, we use wedges, all of us. Chisels are nothing but metal wedges. You drive them into something to split it. An axe head or a hatchet is essentially a metal wedge with a handle to multiply the force while you drive it into a limb or a log. The purpose is simple—to sever and split. Even to destroy. Occasionally humans have even killed each other with them.

So, wedges are powerful little things. And as such they have to be wielded with care. But also consider this—they can make it possible to lift something up, little by little, when you have difficulty doing so the normal way. A wedge can divide, split, destroy. It can lift, hold, help. It all depends on the one who uses it and their purpose.

Wedges are like human words.

Now here is what we have seen this week: a large group of people gathered to express their confusion and disagreement after an election. Most were there like all the groups that come and do this every week at the Capitol. But a considerable number of these people were lit up for action. They came ready to create a violent revolution. This minority included a variety of anarchists and conspiracy theorists, including QAnon, a secretive online community that believes fantastic and delusional things posted—when you read them out loud, they sound insane, which they are. But here is the truth—Christians, even pastors, have been swept up into this cult-like deception. They believed, and have been self-radicalizing online for years, that a secret group of people run the world and that there would be a great event to reveal this and the evildoers would be executed and thrown into prison.

They were prominent among those who crashed inside and roamed the Capitol, even seeking our Vice President to capture and punish him, while lawmakers scrambled for their lives. It was horrid to watch.

But here is the thing—these people, who most of their lives had jobs and families and normal dreams of life, had sat transfixed in chatrooms and online devouring the nonsense, hour after hour. Their brains were filled with conspiracies that don't exist, dragons that need slaying, lies that pounded them until they had no space for truth. They were what I heard someone call "the lied-to."

The people who created this dark world on the web stayed hidden, not because of a cabal of evil but in order to hide whatever their real motive was, probably to make money. Their messages were like little wedges, driven into the wood of people's brains, splitting them off from wives, husbands, work, friends. Over and over, I read these stories in other fringe groups, how an otherwise upstanding person becomes radicalized and obsessed with what the Bible calls a lie. But remember, the Apostle Paul said once, that even Satan disguises himself as an angel of light.

And so, these sons and daughters of ordinary American families, worked into a fevered rage, broke into our shared symbol of democracy, convinced they were saving us all from the very thing they were destroying in the name of a delusional myth.

But this didn't just happen. For a long time, the wedges have been everywhere. Social media and the internet, our own news media across the spectrum from left to right, have been driving the wedges, harder and hard. Our differences are deep if they are all we see. And so, we have pounded them into our common life, harder and harder, and anger gives an energy to drive them deeper than we normally would have.

As we keep driving these wedges, it would be worthwhile to note that wedge words have a limited application. They cannot tie things together or bond that which is separated. Wedges don't heal or feed the hungry. They are not useful for wiping tears and I cannot think of a single joke about wedges that would lift my spirits. They are lowly, mostly limited things. They have their purpose and moments, but not nearly as often as you'd think. I mean, how many logs do you have to split? And how much of your day should be spent propping doors open?

But for a few decades we've been doing that—driving around in our cars listening to people blabbering wedges out to us. You can even choose the wedges you listen to. And reading about wedges on the dark web and bulletin boards.

And all of this brings me to these few words from Jesus. Jesus knew about words. In the Bible, words are everything. God created by His word. Words can bless or curse. Because you can't just fling them out there indiscriminately. They have power, words do. The Hebrews understood this. By "word" the Bible means more than something to use as we please. Jesus is, in fact, Himself the Word of God, that same word by which the world was made, according to the first chapter of John.

The late William Barclay said that by calling Jesus the Word John and the New Testament meant some important things. First, a word is intended to communicate something. In Jesus' case, he proclaimed the gospel, and gave us a message from God. His words were not to hide truth but share it. He brought wisdom, understanding and the gospel.

Second, it is a revelation. In other words, Jesus the Word, is himself an expression of God himself to us. If you want to know what God is like, look here. Be like him. Listen to him. Study his words.

Third, this reveals the larger reason that infuses creation itself. The order, harmony, purpose of the universe is displayed in him. It is not a little secret club of so-called patriots who consign everyone who is not in the club to outer darkness. God's word is revealed in the creation, out where everyone can see it and wonder about it.

Now consider those pitiful wedges again. They push things farther apart while Paul declared "God was in Christ reconciling the world closer together."

All of this brings us to this chilling truth—human words, at best, are a sack of wedges and other limited tools. We ought to use them in the right moment, but they are dangerous when abused or turned into the whole purpose of life. They are words only for us, but unless they do what God wants, they damage God's plan. For God's purposes are not about driving apart but bringing closer, lifting up, and bringing all things into God's great purposes.

When I began working with wedges, I did observe an extraordinary use for them. For three years in my youth, I worked for a bridge company. At that time, we would erect huge logs and set steel beams from one row of logs to another. Then we would build plywood forms and put steel reinforcement bars inside and pour concrete. Then it would dry, and we would remove the forms with crowbars and we had a bridge. Took months to build and some of those bridges are still on Interstate 40 today, but there is another part of this to know.

Before setting the dozens of long steel beams down, row after row, we laid down a wooden board, maybe two feet long, on top of each log. Then we put a row of wooden wedges, as many as 8 on each block facing one way. Then we put an equal number of wedges facing the other direction and laid another board on top of that. Then you set one edge of the steel beam on top of the boards, a kind of wedge sandwich.

It meant every single beam had what we called wedge blocks. Then, when the concrete was dry on the new bridge, we climbed up with sledgehammers and put a hydraulic jack up to the beam and tightened it. Then we started knocking the wedges out. The weight of those forty-foot steel beams settled on the jack instead of the wedges, which fell to the ground. Then we lowered the beam until it could be pulled out and to the ground.

It was dangerous work at every stage. Think of this—hundreds and hundreds of those wedges, facing toward one another, held thousands of pounds of steel and wood and concrete and a crew of men until the bridge was done. The wedges had a purpose—to point toward one another and hold in place and then, its work done, be knocked aside.

The purpose of the bridge was not the wedges. It was to enable people to travel and get across the river or a valley or a low place.

Our words have purposes, but they are not necessarily what God needs. God is building bridges, not splitting logs. God is calling us to work together, not divide into secretive teams that split off. It is time to return our language and wedges back to God's purposes.

I do not know what is to become of this terrible year behind us, but I know that we have made wedges the only tool we seem to have in our country. We keep splitting up, the rhetoric getting harder and angrier. Too many wedges, I'd say. Maybe it's time to face them toward one another and lift something up together for the common good.

And in the Christian church, where we revere words and are terrified lest we misuse them, it may be time to retreat from the wedge throwing hysteria. If we do not show our world how to build bridges and lift burdens, we have damaged the word of God and failed God's purposes. Anger is inevitable but long term it kills.

We are to treat wedges for what they are, not only dangerous when wrongly used, but also sacred in their intentions. We live in a time when all of us have stumbled into the sin of using words too freely, of not waiting and thinking before we speak. We sling them in every direction, faster than we can possibly keep up with them, obsessively sometimes.

Jesus said our words tell who we are. For good or bad. And on the day of judgment, how we deployed our bag of wedges and hatchets, and axes will be brought into the light. Every single word we've uttered will be made accountable. It's a terrifying image.

But another way to see it is this—use the words for life, not death. Eugene Peterson told this story from his ministry:

> When my daughter Karen was young, I often took her with me when I visited nursing homes. She was better than a Bible. The elderly in these homes brightened immediately when she entered the room, delighted in her smile, asked her questions. They would touch her skin, stroke her hair. During one such visit we were with Mrs. Herr, who was in an advanced state of dementia. She was talkative and directed all her talk to Karen. She told her a story, an anecdote out of her childhood that Karen's presence triggered. When she completed her story, she immediately began at the beginning and did it again, word for word and then again and again and again. After twenty minutes or so of this I became anxious lest Karen become uncomfortable and confused about what was going on. So, I interrupted this flow of talk, anointed the woman with oil, laid hands on her, prayed and left. In the car and driving home I commended Karen for her patience and attentiveness. She had listened to this repeated story without showing any sign of restlessness or boredom. I said to her, "Karen, Mrs. Herr's mind is not working the way ours is." And Karen said, "Oh, I knew that Daddy, she was not trying to tell us anything, she was telling us who she is." Nine years old and she knew the difference.[i]

She knew that Mrs. Herr was using words not for communication but for communion. I know what our country needs to do: Have faith in our

Constitution and the idea of a democracy and not give up on it. We are indeed a nation of laws, and we will find our way.

But Christians have another obligation beyond this. It is to speak words of truth and life and reconciliation. We must speak and listen deep, beyond the torrent of empty words and angry words and wedge words and hear who people are. We need to show them the way of Jesus, whose words give life.

Resignation Letter

On the second Sunday of January 2021, I announced my retirement to my congregation after twenty-seven and a half years as their Pastor. I had struggled greatly through the fall with the decision, but finally went to church leaders and asked their guidance. So, the announcement went out, my last day of preaching to be February 28.

Retiring during a pandemic is as strange as everything else in a pandemic. After a ministry that began in the aftermath of a time of enormous conflict in the church prior to my coming, I was voted in and welcomed by a packed church and a standing ovation. It began the happiest and most fulfilling years of my working life. Not every pastor is so fortunate to be so well-matched with a congregation, but ours was a happy partnership. Like all churches, we had conflicts, stresses and more than one person got riled up with me over something, and people left from time to time, as they always do in churches.

More often, though, we worked together, accomplished much, and along the way laughed, cried, loved and prayed together. I did not always do the best, but I always tried my best. My congregation not only loved, appreciated and followed my leadership, they blessed and forgave me for my shortcomings. They are the most remarkable of congregations. So, I include here my resignation statement.

Reinhold Niebuhr was one of the greatest Christian ethicists and theologians of the twentieth century. While many do not know him now, any preacher who has had an education worth anything has read Niebuhr. Several of our Presidents in the past claimed him as an influence. He began his career, though, in a small parish church in Detroit in the 1920s. It was a small congregation, only eighteen families or so, but he ministered among them for thirteen years before leaving for a career of writing and teaching that put him on a larger stage.

He said, at the end of his ministry there that "now that the time has come to sever my connections with the church, I find it almost impossible to do so." (**Leaves from the Notebook of a Tamed Cynic**). That sentence says it for every pastor who ever truly allows himself or herself to plant down and love a congregation. I have been interviewed for a few articles recently and one reporter asked me, "What will you miss the most?" My answer was immediate. "The people, especially children."

When you stay a long time, you have held babies in your arms at the hospital, a day old, and then baptized them, loved them, prayed for them, sometimes long enough to officiate at their wedding. You cry with people, walk in valleys of unimaginable loss, and celebrate extraordinary success alongside them. It is a most honored privilege to walk along with you. Lillian Daniel and Martin Copenhaver called it "this odd and wondrous calling."

Sometimes people have said, "I don't know how you do it." I understand what they are saying—it is stressful and tiring to be around so much of the harder parts of human lives. This work never ends. A life is a work in progress, and I am just part of that journey for you. Whether sermon or visit or just a sentence or two on a Wednesday night or at the grocery store in a chance meeting, this work is always on.

It does indeed wear out a human body and mind, but it also is thrilling. Watching people grow spiritually, overcome their worst failure, or step up into leadership is impossible to convey. Even in death and loss, the privilege of stepping into the Holy of Holies with others, in the place where only God can help, is indescribable. People, hands down, are the best part of all.

So why leave it? Well, I can only say one day *you know*. It is time for someone like me when I was thirty-eight and walked up here that first Sunday to be called here. That was one of the greatest days of our lives, and we have been blessed beyond every expectation. It is time to step back, redirect, do some other things. You know me enough to realize I will find new chapters of ministry and calling. A church is a precious family, and sometimes you move from parent to grandparent. You can still love the children but raising them is not your job anymore.

This is an emotionally hard time to step aside because of the limits of being together, but we will find ways to see each other and say things. We will continue to belong to this church as it is appropriate and timely to do so. And You have great leaders here. Trust in each other. It is a changing time, and what God has up ahead will be great. This is a wonderful, healthy church.

I have done all that I was able to do. And you are fortunate indeed that you got my incredible wife in the process. There is nothing I have done that would have been possible without Vickie Johnson Furr. She is the most admirable and talented person I have ever known. So, with profound gratitude, we will enjoy these weeks. Your leadership has been working on a process for the interim time. You will be okay. You have a solid and wonderful staff. Help them, hold them up, pray for them. I love you and look forward to great days ahead.

Now, we have six weeks ahead and work to do. Let's treasure the time together we have!

Pastoral Prayer
January 17, 2021, MLK Holiday Weekend

Eternal God, You did not only create religion and church people
You made everyone.
You do not only love some of us, but all of us.
You did not only send Jesus for a failed mission for the few
But in a bold, audacious claim upon us all.
You are working not only in the sacred and spiritual
But also in the rough and tumble of world events,
The compromised shadows of politics and warfare,
In the sweep of global economy and in the tiniest family pain.
When we are doing our worst, You are often turning it on its head
    To make something unbelievably good out of our broken choices.
You are Lord not only of our public confession but our private struggles.
You call us again when we are sure we are beyond loving
And heal us sometimes when we did not even realize
    The depth of our disease.
Today we come and pray for the nations
    As well as for this nation.
We are grateful to live in this country.
We thank You for those and their families who defend us with their lives,
We pray today for America to remember her best truths.
We pray for our leaders
For President elect Joe Biden and his wife, for Kamala Harris and her
    husband
For outgoing President Trump and his family, and for our Congress
In this moment, help us to follow Your leadership
And for all leaders across the world, that they might hear Your claims
    Upon their leadership, their hearts, and their ambitions
May they do what is right, not only what gives right appearances.
Be with the least and the most vulnerable—
    The children of our world, their families,
    Those shattered by war and ravaged by hunger
    Victims of fraud and greed with punctured dreams
    The homeless and those struggling to stay in a home
    The unemployed and workers living amid anxious rumors
    And the layoffs of friends and their families

For the lonely, the heartsick, and the hardened rebels
Who ignore Your call to their own peril.

Help us who claim to be Your people
> Live up to the name not only with zeal and passion
> But also principle and careful thought.

May we be good stewards of material blessings, freedom, the gospel
> And the relationships in our lives. In Jesus' name.

As the nation continued to reel over the events of January 6 and the deep divisions between us, I wrote these reflections about the path ahead. I chose, finally, not to post these to the church. I had already shared concerns and prayers since those events. And in light of my resignation and imminent retirement, I chose to keep these as private reflections. It seems now, in looking back, that they are true as ever. Democracy is a beautiful and powerful set of ideas. But they are not impervious to human negligence or wickedness. At a moment when trust in institutions and confusion about the very notion of public truth brought into question, I share these thoughts. They are mine and represent only me. But I believe they are right.

Martin Luther King Day,
January 18, 2021

A Church in a Divided Land….

In this moment, National Guardsmen, Secret Service agents and the FBI are scouring the nation, trying to find people still bent on sending us into anarchy. Whatever they think about themselves, it is clear that our troubles have escalated to a terrible place. The mob last week came within a minute of face-to-face contact with Vice President Pence as they chanted to hang him as a traitor. They broke into Speaker Pelosi's office, intent on bringing her out to some absurd notion of a frontier trial and who knows what else. It was a traumatic moment. Officers and rioters died, and many were injured. We were all traumatized.

In elections, people win, and people lose. As long as we trust one another—and that is the reality, given that elections are carried out by thousands of organized volunteers—we live with it. Now, though, in a time when we each self-select the interpretations of facts that we will listen to and believe only those, most of us are disconnected from the ability to hear the whole story. There are groups at the extreme edges of our divisions that constantly push their perceived grievances until people are motivated to act. When those people begin to act—loot, burn, shoot and kill—democracy itself is at risk. The democratic way is fragile and strong at the same time. Fragile in that it doesn't take long for it to be done away, strong in that if we believe in it, nothing can destroy it. As Senator Mitt Romney said, profoundly, last week, "The way to respect voters who think the election was stolen is tell them the truth."

His statement was so obvious, so childlike in its simplicity, but it was the best word of the day to me. In a church, in a town, in a neighborhood homeowners association, telling the truth is the only antidote to conflict. It is painful and hard, but eventually things get better. There will be another election in two years, and another Presidential election in four. We have everything to motivate our staying together but seem to have little interest in doing so.

The undercurrents are strong—people are fraying at the edges of their ability to cope. The pandemic and our government response, racial tensions last summer that eventuated in 14,000 arrests, continuous conflict over policing and race, the stress and strain on our law enforcement system, along with constant debates over toxic issues. And among the various tribes of our nation, our resentments grow as our leaders are megaphones for our own worse impulses instead of leading us.

This is not going to be easy. But it has to start with leaders, all leaders. We desperately need the truth. Pursuing justice and truth among our national leaders matters. But it needs to start in the churches as well. I have been watching Christian groups drift farther and deeper into the toxins and become part of the problem. If we don't lead by our own example, how can we speak any word to the world around us?

"Tell the truth." You have to stop whatever else you're doing and do that. And that means we have to start to ferret it out from the tsunami of misinformation and self-promotion that streams into our phones and homes and lives. Political leaders, church leaders, community leaders, and parents, we need to make truth our top priority. I can tell you this: it won't be swift, and it won't be easy to digest. Lies don't have to take any time, since you don't need facts. Just make it up, or let your emotions persuade. Truth, though, takes time. You investigate, follow process, you listen, you wait, you dig all the way down. Only there will you get past simplistic slogans and subjective emotions. Just tell the truth. Jesus said, "Let your yes mean yes, and your no mean no."

Oh, and one more difficult part of this: You must tell yourself the truth. For many people this will be almost impossible. They too easily have settled on a patch of what they believe and refuse to listen any longer. If we're going to get out of this with a democracy, we're going to have to put our emotional shotguns back on the gun rack and open the door. Start by calming down.

Try to tell yourself the truth, and if you don't know, allow yourself a few questions and some more perspectives to help you.

McDonald's Drive-Through
January 20, 2021

She is young and pretty
I can tell even behind the
Dirty glass and the face mask.
Her smooth caramel skin
and youthful eyes contain a
whole world I don't have time to find.

"Did you bring Your best smile today?" I ask
And she grins. Even behind that mask
I can tell it is a beautiful smile.

"I bet you'll need it. There will be some
grumpy people coming today.
"Oh yes sir, they always be there."
She beams, and I take my receipt.
I pull forward, get my food, and go.

It is a little game I play of pleasantries
with people in cages, drive-throughs,
parking decks and jail cells. Somehow
a smile seems a small gift to offer.

Pastoral Prayer
The Spiritual Journey January 24, 2021

Blessed God, Father, Son and Spirit
Who surrounds us with the mystery of Creation
      and Your mighty care for all You have made
The wonder of Salvation
and the comfort of Presence and transformation,
We come today to ask and to intercede
      Not merely to answer our wishes or indulge our feelings
But to call us from places of comfort into places of growth
We are in times full of challenge and anxiety
Uncertainty and possibility.
Teach us again to "Fear Not" in the face of the unfamiliar
And to trust You in midst of the unknown.
We pray this day for our nation
We have watched a new President and administration begin their work
even as the wounds of the election are still with us.
As he takes up his work as steward of this nation.
We pray that changes in our nation
continue to find ways of peace and reconciliation
We are also glad that the durability of our faith in every season sustains us.

We thank You for all who serve us and ask Your blessings on them for
Wisdom and humility and the spirit of a servant.
Guide us all to do what is right, help where it is needed,
pray without ceasing and cease from anger.
We ask Your blessing for doctors, nurses, support workers,
and all those who care for the sick,
Especially now, that You help them not merely to do their work
But to sustain them in the face of unimaginable grief, loss and sadness.
Sustain their souls, keep them from despair, and protect them.
Bless our economic lives together,
give wisdom and guidance to bankers, legislators, financial leaders,
community leaders, factory owners, business entrepreneurs,
Investors, boards, suppliers, builders, and people who sell.
Bless our economic life, which is so essential not only to us
but all the world, we ask for a new sense of urgency and accountability.
Be with our public health and political leaders

And those tasked with the implementation of a vaccine
May we all help out, pitch in, be patient,
and offer up our conveniences for someone else.
Help us to remember our connections to each other
And our obligations to all for righteousness, kindness, and responsibility.
You have given us all we need.
Help us to give all that we ought.

Now as Your church, most of all, make us good stewards
of the gospel of Jesus.
Not merely in our talking, but by living it as Jesus did, as followers unafraid
But also radiant with the True Love of Christ
That welcomes, abides, and changes.
Now for this Your church,
we pray for wisdom in days ahead as they seek a new pastor together
and care for one another in that journey.
As we continue to hold together for the joyous hope of being together again,
and rejoicing in our gathered life, help us.
On this journey of spiritual change, speak to us
Draw us nearer, prick our consciences, break our hearts
Humble us from pride, rebuke our sins, forgive our guilt
Heal our wounds, not that we would be as we were
But that we might see You and love You and please You
More and better and more faithfully. Amen.

Pastoral Prayer for Guidance
January 31, 2021

Eternal God
with the coming of Jesus
the chasm of sin that estranged us from Your love was overcome.
With the coming of the Spirit, we replaced
the boundaries that separated us by language, culture, geography and politics
with forgiveness, connection and Christian fellowship.
You asked us to call You friend.
So, we come this day as long-lost family,
here together in this moment only by our inner lives
and heartfelt presence.

We give thanks for our church, for our fellowship,
and for our common love in Christ.
Today we ask that You give us
loving hearts, keen minds, teachable spirits and steady faith.
Amid this culture damaged by lies, mistrust and disinformation,
inspire us to live closer to You,
and to love one another with our whole hearts.

Remind us of the things that matter.
Free us to live more simply.
In these times of inconvenience, risk and separation,
show us how to live in contentment and peace
because we have chosen the better things.

We pray for families, churches, and leaders everywhere
that they remain calm and steadfast.
We pray for those on the front lines of life, healing,
and at the same time risking everything to do so.
Even as too many in their distrust and anger make their work harder
we pray today to be salt and light where we are.

Lord, we are embarking as a church on a new time.
Vickie and I enter a new and unknown adventure.
Our beloved church enters into a time requiring patience, discernment,
and trust in each other.

Guide them, and us, in this time.
Keep us together, keep us true, keep us centered on Jesus.
Bless our church and its people.
This day we pray for a hurting world--
the lost, the lonely, the alienated, the afraid, the angry, the hopeless.
Help us see them and not react against them
but welcome them into the arms of gospel love.

Help us to make a continuing difference for the Kingdom.
Fill us with the joy and enthusiasm of spiritual renewal
and remind us that in all times and places, we can be faithful to You.
May our mutual faith be deepened.
May our church grow more powerful
by humble surrender to Your guidance and will.
May our suffering be changed into surrender and transformation,
and new hope.
May our homes be saved from the principalities and powers
of economy, power, desire and politics
and our discipleship lead us to good stewardship of our lives and each other.

May our witness be strong and our faith be renewed,
and our commitments not waiver.
May our children follow in our example and our example be worth following.
May our generosity and partnerships with all of Your people grow
and change us forever.
May we have courage in our living and confidence in our dying.
All of this we pray in the great name of Jesus Christ,
Word become flesh and dwelling among us, full of grace and truth. Amen.

Pastoral Prayer
February 7, 2021

Mighty God
If we do not always grasp the greatness of the life that is within us,
    The wonder of this glorious world where we live it,
    if we fail to sing and laugh and give thanks for
    the gift even of being here, breathing, eating, sleeping, loving
        and playing,
    it is because we become numb by routine and false security.
    and in these days worn thin by too much worry, too little certainty
    too much triviality and too little wisdom,
We are distracted by our daily lives and disruptions,
    and absorbed in what is nearest to us rather than what is most
    important.
But much of our lack of thankfulness may lie in lives that are
    over-programmed, over-stressed, over-scheduled and
    overwhelmed.
Our minds are clouded with too much information
    our hearts are loaded with too many concerns
Our bodies are wracked with anxiety as well as disease
    and the threat of a virus that can take life in a week.
So, we come to this day with a desire to move into thankfulness
to leave behind worries and troubles which are ever near
and be in these moments more aware of You, more grateful to You
more ready to know You better and more hunger to love You.
We look forward to stopping, resting, and being with people we love.
Help us to turn our minds away from these things
    and toward You.
If we are self-absorbed, help us to see the needs of others around us
If we are distracted, grant that we would find depth of commitment
    so that our lives might know the joy of focused purpose.
If we continue looking to the past, help us to see what is here, now,
    waiting for us.
Fill our hearts with new vision
    so that we might count our blessings instead of complaining
    about our challenges.
    and offer our gratitude for this free nation, its great heritage,
and its resilience and strength.

Grant us patience and strength of national character today
      to advocate what is right and best and not merely expedient.
In the strong name of Jesus, Amen.

As I began my work at Vestavia Hills Baptist Church in 1993 in the aftermath of a difficult and painful division in the church and led them to heal and be renewed, I parted during a pandemic, with a drive-by reception outside, where members could leave notes and cards, and wave to us. There were fewer than eighty to hear the final sermon. I came in with a bang, and left, as T. S. Elliot put it, with a whimper. It probably served me right, as Baptist preachers are especially prone to spiritual pride in numbers. But the creative month of celebration and appreciation was anything but small. I could not have asked for better for me and for my wife and family.

I was especially appreciative during this final season of my partner and wife, Vickie, whose many years of work in the congregation left her fingerprints everywhere. She detests the spotlight, but in leading a project to involve others and accomplish something she is unparalleled. She left behind a Sunday School class that was outstanding in fellowship and generosity, a hospitality house that she oversaw and cared for as we welcomed missionaries, pastors from other nations, ministers in crisis and young interns and staff serving our church and other places. She renovated and redecorated homes and lives all over our church and beyond, her special gift. The congregation not only mourned my leaving but also hers.

More than once since leaving, I have missed the joy of being a full time pastor. What to preach as You end Your time with people You love? I chose to end my forty-one years as a pastor by preaching on love—love of God, of neighbor, of enemies, of truth. In an insane moment when every thread of our social existence was frayed, it turned out to be exactly what we needed. It seemed to me to be the highest peak of the many mountains of scripture and the Christian tradition. It is somewhere to be found in all the religions of the world, overtly or implied, and at the heart of ethics, justice and all that is worthwhile in personal life.

Here is the sermon preached at the end of that series, on my next to the last Sunday in the pulpit as the pastor of Vestavia Hills Baptist Church. Preached on the first Sunday of Lent, February 21, 2021.

"Love One Another"
John 13:1-15, 31-35; 15:1-12

It seems so simple. "We just need to love one another." And, in a way, it *is* simple. This is clearly the highest aspect of the Christian faith. Nothing seems to compete with these commands to love. All else pales when we think of love. It is easy enough to judge religious ideas that claim truth but do not have love. They may be impressive. They may be full of fire and persuasion. They may even grow in vast numbers. But they are not finally Christian, for when we see to their core what we find is hatred or anger or egotism or corporate pride. Not love. We know that love is the defining quality of our common faith. Love for God, love for our neighbor, love for each other.

Yet the real problem is not *that* we are to love. We know that. It's like saying, "What really counts is to be happy in life." People spend billions of dollars trying, but saying it isn't the same as *being* happy. The question is, "How *can* I be happy?"

Love can be deceptive, too. What we call love may not be. It can be a sentimental, unrealistic feeling-oriented understanding that operates by denial. The unwritten rule is, "We have to feel good about one another. We can never disagree. We can never feel negative emotions. We can never debate or discuss things. To do so is to risk falling out of fellowship."

Such an arrangement may be pleasant, but it is not love. So what is? Here we read two "love commands" of Jesus. Surprisingly, these are not given to us about loving the world or our kinfolk or even our enemies (though Jesus told us to love all of these elsewhere!). The command here is to love our fellow Christians.

Several years ago, an editor compiled a book in which some of our greatest living secular writers gave their perspectives on Christianity. Many were unbelievers. Oddly, most of their objections about Christianity were not about doctrinal matters like the Second Coming or Hell or even the issue of why there is suffering in the world. Their biggest concern? "Why don't Christians look more like Christ?" It could be put like this: if Jesus set forth a religion of love and forgiveness, and commissioned his followers to be the embodiment of that ethic of love and forgiveness, why doesn't the church act more like Jesus told them to act?

Chapter 13 is set in the upper room, at the time of the Last Supper before Jesus was to die. Jesus therefore told the disciples that *they must follow his example*. The imitation of Christ is an old and honored part of the Christian heritage. Yet when we look at the teachings and life of Jesus today, we find a puzzling reality. For some strange reason, we have managed to explain away the need for imitating Jesus in our lives.

Something must live in us in a more than superficial way for it to be a conviction. Convictions are that which, if they were taken from our lives, would make us a different person. Convictions are not interchangeable with new concepts or ideas. They are part of who we are. To lose them is to enter a grief process.

What are our deepest convictions? Convictions, you see, are revealed not by our words but by our living. And what does our life path tell about us?

And maybe when it comes to our faith, we have watered down this life to something like this: *Jesus is admirable, but no one can really live a life like that in the real world. It just doesn't work.* You get crucified if you do.

Listen, do you know why Christians don't look more like Christ? Because we have too much of the world's agenda in us. We are living in the midst of a competitive and power-hungry world. To survive and thrive in it, you have to play by the world's rules. You do not always get rewarded for doing what is right. So we often make ways to "get around" this difficulty.

Many Christians don't actually like each other. We see this on the largest level among denominations. A Baptist minister was summoned to the bedside of a Presbyterian woman who was quite sick. As he went up the sidewalk to the house, he met the little daughter of the woman and said, "I'm very glad your mother wanted to call on me in this time of need. Is your pastor out of town?" "No," said the little girl, "He's at home, but we thought she might have something contagious and didn't want to expose him to it."

These denominational differences are breaking down, but our disunity continues to say to the world, "Christians don't really love one another." And it happens in congregations as well. Factions, divisions, disunity, are everywhere. This essential failure is striking.

I would venture to say it is worse after this past year, because the divisions of our culture—political, racial and economic—have been laid bare in front of us. We can't pretend we're on the same teams. We aren't. Unless we choose to be on Jesus' team.

So how do we overcome this dilemma? I mean, it just seems to be in the cards, given all these human beings in the church. And here we learn one crucial aspect of becoming a disciple. *We have to let go.* In v. 3, Jesus is fully aware of his authority and standing before God. Yet he rose from supper and "laid aside" his garments and began to wash the disciple's feet. Jesus' act is a prophetic enactment of his coming death, not an allusion to baptism, the Lord's Supper or the institution of a new ordinance of foot-washing. We have not continued to practice "foot washing," except on rare occasions. We say it is because it no longer holds great meaning to modern people, but perhaps it is because it gets on our last nerve, too close and too hard.

A clue can be found in verse 4. The word for "took off" or "laid aside" is the same word Jesus spoke in 10:15: "I *lay down* my life for the sheep." Jesus willingly lays aside every claim to greatness in the worldly sense to be obedient to the cross.

The washing of the dusty feet of guests in Palestine was a lowly act, to be performed by a slave, or by the wife of the host if no servant was available. The disciples expected to wash the Master's feet, but how could they comprehend this?

To love one another we have to "lay aside" some things. Let them go. We lay aside our claims of superiority or importance. We lay aside our need to always be right, to always make the decisions, to always control the plans or the money or the outcome. Jesus had every right to reject his own disciples after the resurrection: one betrayed him, another denied him, and the rest forsook him on the cross and ran away. Jesus released his claim and instead forgave them so that he might show them another way.

It is this "letting go" that makes real community at least possible. Sometimes this letting go can be quite painful, for it means seeing the truth about ourselves. *We have to let go.*

But that is not all. *We also have to* "take hold of something." The second requirement that we find rooted in these identical settings of the love commandment is that we are to *be rooted in the living presence of the risen Christ.* This we know by the presence of the Holy Spirit in our lives.

We see that in this second setting of the love commandment that Jesus gives us about our life together as a Christian community that it is set in the context of his discourse on the vine and the branches. In other words, the fruit of love in our lives is closely tied to our rootedness in Jesus.

This is not to say that we are incapable of love in our human lives on our own. Love is at the heart of human existence—we could not live without it. Our tendency, however, is to love those who love us and stay away from those who don't. Jesus called us to something more difficult: to find a way to love one another even when it isn't easy. And the way we do that is not by somehow solving our differences or by one of us caving in to the other.

Our fellowship cannot survive if it is based only on a surface impression or appearances. Real community involves getting deeper than the surface. We have to meet Christ in one another, and that will only happen as we engage each other at a level of depth. And it will only survive if we are "rooted" spiritually in the living Christ.

That is why the fellowship of the church is ultimately a spiritual question, not a matter of programs or how much we are alike or even whether we like each other. It is a matter of letting go and holding on. Letting go of our worldly entitlements, our reputations, our pride, our sins, our resentments, our anger, and our need to control. And holding on to Jesus, deeper and deeper until he gets into control of us. And when he has control, he can begin to change us. Deep enough so that whenever we recognize him inside another, no matter how repugnant they might be, or sick or broken, we love him there.

Love, Paul says, is actually superior to either faith or hope, because both will one day be done away with, but not love. Love is what alone will survive into eternity. Love is the very nature of God and thus is eternal.

This is an audacious claim, I think, that love is at the heart of life, the universe and all that we are. It is common to talk about hope today, about the promise of heaven and eternal life. But what is more important is love. Paul says it this way:

1 Corinthians 13:13 And now faith, hope, and love abide, these three; and the greatest of these is love. And in 1 Corinthians 13:8 Love never ends.

This does not merely mean sentiment, as in, "I will always love you," *but that there is something indestructible, permanent, foundational about love.* It undergirds and holds the other two. If it isn't the final truth, faith and hope collapse.

That is Paul's point here. That we do not get it means that we do not understand either hope or love very well.

When all else is gone, love will live on. The question is, will we? And the answer is, "It all depends." If we spend our lives invested in eternal love, we will share eternity. If we build lives on anything else—fear, hate, getting rich at the expense of all else, control, you name your own list—it will simply vanish at the last.

So, I suppose the same is true for a church or humanity. Eternal love or everything else?

So here is my word for us today: love one another. Ok, the world is messed up badly right now, but it's also full of hidden love, divine moments everywhere. Go to those, live into them, practice this, live against the cruelties of this time. Believe in it, no matter what else others say. Stay out of the rabbit holes of endless distractions and arguments. Love one another.

And as you search for the new shepherd for this flock, here is my advice. It's yours, you're still paying for my advice for a little longer, so here it is: resist the temptation to reinvent yourselves. There will be a thousand pathways that promise some new or exciting or untried formula for church success. They don't really work, not for long. You cannot have a church made of gimmicks and mirrors and pr tricks. It's not about becoming something you aren't. But it is about staying together, loving one another, trusting each other.

You do not have to have the answers to everything to be a church. But you do have to love one another. If you continue in that love and stay together, You will find the answers you need for the days ahead and the fast-changing world we're all living through.

Bernard of Clairvaux, an ancient Christian leader, once wrote that when we seek knowledge for the sake of knowledge, we are indulging our curiosity. Curiosity about the world has given us scientific knowledge and solved many problems of human life. Curiosity, we often say, "killed the cat," but without it very little would change. Curiosity can be good—and it can be not so good. Just because we can do something doesn't mean it is good. Curiosity has its limits.

Others, said Bernard, desire to know in order that they may themselves be known. This "knowing" leads to vanity. Yet even this most superficial way of knowing is not devoid of benefits for the world. A scientist is driven by the desire for fame to achieve a breakthrough in medical technology. Her motives are not pure, but the end result is still one that is positive. But there comes with vanity the temptation to do less than our best, or to fail to do the best when there is nothing "in it for us."

There is a third kind of seeker of knowledge, said Bernard. It is the one who seeks knowledge "in order to serve and edify others: and that is love." Love alone can continue to persist amid boredom, weariness, discouragement and unrewarding circumstances. Love can complete its task out of devotion to the object of its affection.

Curiosity might take on the task as long as it is interesting. Vanity might do it as long as it holds the promise of a payoff. But love takes it on because it must be done for the sake of another whose happiness is greater than love's own.

Curiosity and vanity have something to give the self. Love has a self to give. Therein lies all the difference in the world.

You can be a church that does great things. Sometimes a church can be renowned for its programs and vast resources. It solves every kind of problem it can identify and meets every need on the map.

A church can also be famous. Its preacher might be famous or its members important in their community. It is "the" place to go for a while until the next one comes along.

But a church that matters is aiming to teach the love of Jesus, how to be like Him, practice his way, and live in love. This is what I hope to leave with you as I go. Put this at the center of your life together. The world needs it, and so do we.

Heaven's Gate
March 4, 2021

It had to be a dream
Because I am still here--
I suddenly stood in line
At the entrance door to Paradise.

The crowd reminded me
Of the last time that I toured
The loud dirty streets of old Jerusalem
Priests, soldiers, beggars and tourists wall to wall.

I was at the back of the line.
The man who was in charge
Made our assignments so we would
Know what we'd do when we went in.

A man in a motorized wheelchair
With twisted limbs and stooping neck
Was sent to an Olympic stadium
To run against the wind.

A woman bruised and eyes downcast
Was told she now was free
To study and to roam the cosmos
And go just where she pleased without her husband.

Children who had died young
And those who were afflicted
Were announced to be judges and
To sit next to Jesus.

On and on the assignments set
The earthly stations inside out.
Doctors, nurses, scholars and mechanics.
People from Paris and carpenters from down South.

I was with preachers, kings and Presidents
Celebrities and billionaires
The ones who got to run the Earth
Whose words went everywhere

We waited, first expectantly,
Then a sense of dread
Criminals and homeless bums
Heard their names called instead.

But finally, after many hours
and only we remained
The Man in charge gestured us
And called out all our names.

"A gift is best," we heard him say
"When it is something you really need."
So, I'll give you something for your life
That bound to set you free."

"The children will deliver you
To a green space far away,
No one there to listen
Or worship what you say."

"And there you may be silent
As long as you require
To liberate yourselves from fame
And the prison of desire."

Of course, we were deflated.
The others we had watched
Were given their true hearts' desires
And we, it seemed, had not.

But he smiled as he sent us out
And my dream ended just then
Before I reached that meadow where
My restless soul would end.

Now I try hard to remember
The parts I want to keep
As I woke up to the real world
Or perhaps fell back asleep.

Every Time I Think of You
(to all who every prayed for me)

I tried to fly above the angels
With nothing but self-centeredness
But I only found the way to heaven
From wandering in the wilderness

I took this road a long time ago
Without knowing where it went
When I thought I'd lost my way,
I felt the prayers you sent

CHORUS:
I thank God when I think of you
You are a gift to me
Of faithfulness and hope and love
      and generosity

For all my sins and weaknesses
I now feel gratitude
Without them I might never have known
How much I needed you.

When fear and anger silence truth,
And mercy is ridiculed as weak,
I remember you still pray for me
And I find my voice and speak.

My Final Column

All good things must come to an end, said the bard. So be it. I had one last sermon to preach, one last visit to make, one final meeting to attend, and one final column to write for the newsletter. This is it.

This is my final column as the pastor of Vestavia Hills Baptist Church. We were musing together during staff meeting how many of these little columns I have written. We switched to "bi-monthly" years ago but for years I cranked out one of these pieces every week. I have somewhere north of 800 columns filed in this folder on my computer just in my time here.

These little writings occasionally were good enough to turn into a sermon later, or at least a desperate Wednesday night devotional or a meditation for the Thursday communion in the chapel for so many years. It was really a "what's on my mind, and I hope yours, too."

I began writing a column the way I do during my years in South Georgia. In my early years as a pastor, I read the book **The Tender Shepherd** by John Killinger. He said too many pastors squander the opportunity to communicate with their congregation on a substantive level by simply writing promotional blather in their newsletter. He made it his practice for much of his ministry to try to write something significant, helpful, and spiritually encouraging. It gave me the image of talking to one person when you write, as though we were sitting across the kitchen table from one another drinking coffee and having unhurried conversation.

I would write about what was on my mind even as I always managed to work in whatever I was supposed to promote-- the budget, the next big program, or why you needed to get back into regular church attendance after being at the beach and the lake all summer. But it was also a dialogue. I would share what I had been reading or thinking about. Often, I was responding to conversations still on my mind with members.

In these pages I celebrated with you, tried to speak of our common griefs, confessed when we were undone together by the world around us, and rejoiced in our victories and accomplishments together. And I realize that I was sharing bits and pieces of our family with you as we parented with you, then launched our children and entered grandparenting. When I went to see older members in assisted care or in their homes, I discovered that they read this faithfully and it was a way to be in touch with their church and pastor.

I wrote about what was present and ongoing with our life together. And always, I wrote in response to you. I had faces and situations in my heart. I would think about what you were going through. And sometimes, as in 9-11 and other events, we were all wounded.

It has been a true joy and privilege to serve here and to do this work. Sometimes people will say sympathetic things to preachers like, "I don't know how pastors do what they do." My reply is, "Oh, it is the greatest job in the world. I enjoy almost every aspect of it. The problem is there's just so much of it." That's why you can't do it forever.

One of the pleasures I have permitted myself lately is to look back, to sift and savor. And because there is so much to remember, these columns are my markers. When I re-read them, or a sermon, or an email I saved, I pull up people's faces, and stories and laughter and tears.

It's been a great ride with you. I have the records saved for reflection—sermons, eulogies, journal entries, columns, emails. I have been privileged to walk it along with my wife, Vickie, whose own ministry is lived out in deeds and caring, and encouragement is one of my great inspirations in life. She is an extraordinary wife, mother, teacher, grandmother, and fellow minister. Her impact on my life and others is enormous. I am grateful for her, as you are.

Thank you for loving me, letting me lead, following, praying for us, caring for our children and grandchildren and us, and being with us. I am hopeful about the future of our church and the church. This last year has created a heartache of longing for being together again. It is probably just what we all needed, virus aside, to remember how meaningful human fellowship is.

I know and like Bill Owen a lot. As he comes, you will like him too. Make a little room for him as he helps you. He brings a lifetime of experience and knowledge about church and transitions. And start praying for your next pastor now, even before anyone has a clue who it will be. Let go of what you think the church ought to do and start asking God to guide you together.

Most of all, I am grateful to God, about Whom I have thought about every day throughout the day as long as I remember. God's mysterious and gentle and faithful Presence has given us grace, persevered with our failings, and blessed our feeblest effort.

God bless you all.

Gary

Now, all these months later, I end with this short song lyric, written just before the death of my precious mother-in-law. It seems fitting for an ending. I hope you, reader, might have been uplifted, helped to ponder, or weep for something hard and difficult, or led to a deeper life by a word or verse. Thank you for listening. Three quarters of a million of our fellow Americans died of the virus, millions more were sick and all of us grieved. Not to mention the entire rest of humanity. It was a somber time, but gratitude never requires favorable conditions—only acknowledgement. Life is a gift. Open it thankfully..

Farewell
October 1, 2021, for Betty

The moment comes to say goodbye,
You don't want it to end--
We've reminisced about old times,
And talked about old friends.
But it's getting dark, and my car is parked
A good way from here.
But first I have some things to say
I've carried them for years.

Chorus:
Thanks for your hospitality
You always fed us well.
Parting is indeed sweet sorrow
Farewell, my friend, farewell.

Old folks used to stand and wave
Until their guests disappeared.
Now folks rush back in the house like
We were never really here.
        So, I pause to say I love you now,
Though I know you understand.
I'll treasure all you did for us
Until we meet again…

Thanks for your hospitality
You always fed us well.
Parting is indeed sweet sorrow
Farewell, my friend, farewell.

Notes

Barclay, William. ***Jesus As They Saw Him***. Harper and Row; Book Club (BCE/BOMC) edition (January 1, 1962).

Hardin, H. Grady; Quillian, Joseph; White, James F., ***The Celebration of the Gospel: A Study in Christian Worship***, (Abingdon Press, 1964)

Peterson, Eugene. "Novelists, Pastors And Poets," ***Crux***, 26 no 4. December 1990, p 3-9.

Reis Thebault, Tim Meko and Junne Alcantara, "Sorrow and Stamina, Defiance and Despair: It's Been a Year." The Washington Post, March 11, 2021.

Wetzler, Robert & Huntington, Helen. ***Seasons & Symbols: A Handbook on the Church Year***
(Minneapolis: Augsburg Publishing, 1962).